With tha

142nd c,

celebra

Portadown Corps.

God bless you both in your
ongoing leadership and
ministry.

29/01/23

One-Minute
PRAYERS®

for
LEADERS

Steve Miller

HARVEST HOUSE PUBLISHERS
EUGENE, OREGON

Cover design by Bryce Williamson
Cover photo © SpicyTruffel

One-Minute Prayers® for Leaders
Copyright © 2021 by Steve Miller
Published by Harvest House Publishers
Eugene, Oregon 97408
www.harvesthousepublishers.com

ISBN 978-0-7369-8001-2 (hardcover)
ISBN 978-0-7369-8002-9 (eBook)

Printed in China

21 22 23 24 25 26 27 28 29 / RDS-CD / 10 9 8 7 6 5 4 3 2 1

CONTENTS

———

PART 1

MY CULTIVATION
AS A LEADER

LEADING BY EXAMPLE

Lord, during Your ministry on Earth, You led by example. In all that You did, You were a perfect role model of good leadership. You took a group of ordinary followers and turned them into extraordinary leaders.

Today, Your example continues to inspire. May I look to You and learn from You. As I consider what made You a great leader, I think of Your faithfulness, love, humility, patience, wisdom, grace, and even forgiveness. All that stands in contrast to the worldly perspective, which says leadership is about exercising authority, displaying charisma, and achieving goals. You made it clear that a good leader is a person of good character. In Your Word, when You describe what is required of a leader, You talk only about a person's internal qualities—not external accomplishments.

As I seek to lead others, Lord, may I imitate Your character qualities. May I pay attention not only to what You said and did, but *how* You did it—so that I too may lead by example.

Those who say they live in God
should live their lives as Jesus did.

1 JOHN 2:6 NLT

STARTING THE DAY RIGHT

Father, when I fail to start the day with You, things get chaotic fast. When I tackle my to-do list without consulting You first, I end up doing things in my own strength instead of Yours.

Like the psalmist, may I come to You with eagerness "in the morning…and wait expectantly" (Psalm 5:3 NIV). Starting my day in Your presence really does make a difference. When I spend time with You and ask for a new supply of Your wisdom and peace, then I approach my day with God-confidence instead of self-confidence.

All through the hours of my work, Lord, may I stay close to You. Make me sensitive to Your leading so that I don't stray from Your plans for Me. I know You want what is best for me. The sooner I am in Your presence each day, the sooner I can tune my heart to Yours.

My voice You shall hear in the morning, O LORD;
In the morning I will direct it to You,
And I will look up.

PSALM 5:3

WHERE GREAT LEADERSHIP STARTS

Lord, when I read Your Word, sometimes I'm quicker to think about how it applies to my personal life rather than how it can guide me as a leader. As I ponder Your truths, promises, and commands, may I take time to consider how they can shape the way I lead.

Within Scripture I see many examples of how devotion to Your Word is vital for great leadership. Because Joshua meditated upon and obeyed Your commands, You honored him with military victories. Because David hid Your Word in his heart, he became a prosperous king. Because of Nehemiah's love for Your precepts, he was effective in stirring up an apathetic people to rebuild the fallen walls of Jerusalem in just 52 days.

Your Word, Lord, is the starting point to success in every area of life, including leadership. That's why I want to make it the foundation of all I do. As I spend time in my Bible, may I listen carefully to what You want to teach me.

This Book of the Law shall not depart from your mouth,
but you shall meditate in it day and night, that you may
observe to do according to all that is written in it.
For then you will make your way prosperous,
and then you will have good success.

JOSHUA 1:8-9

ALWAYS ROOM FOR GROWTH

Lord, may I always see myself as having room to grow as a leader. Instill within me a humble spirit that earnestly seeks to learn and get better at what I do. May I not fall into the trap of becoming prideful about my accomplishments, for then I will stop growing—both as a leader, and in my reliance upon You to help me lead well.

When it comes to my leadership, may I have the same attitude as the apostle Paul, who wrote, "One thing I do: forgetting what lies behind and straining forward to what lies ahead, I press on toward the goal for the prize of the upward call of God in Christ Jesus" (Philippians 3:13-14 ESV).

As I begin each day, may I do so with a prayer that asks, "Open my eyes to the things I need to learn so I may excel as a leader."

I pray that the eyes of your heart may be enlightened
in order that you may know the hope
to which he has called you.

EPHESIANS 1:18 NIV

God's Constant Presence

Thank You, Father, for Your promise that You are with me at all times. The assurance of Your presence gives me peace and confidence as I make my way through each day. When I need wisdom, You are just a prayer away. When I need help, I am reminded that with Your provision I can do all things. When difficulties arise, I know You are my Great Shepherd—even to the point of walking with me through the valley of death.

I can count on You to be faithful even when I am not. Your Spirit within me is my guide as I seek to follow You. Your grace is sufficient for me; I will never run out of it. In my weaknesses, Your strength shines.

Because You are steadfast, I have nothing to fear. My heart and mind can rest because in You, I lack nothing. Thank You, Lord, for being my everything.

The LORD is my shepherd; I shall not want.

PSALM 23:1

SEEKING GOD FIRST

Father, life is so chaotic! I am surrounded by the noise of busyness all the time. The static from all the demands competing for my attention makes it difficult for me to listen to Your still, small voice. Unless I make a deliberate effort to set aside quiet and undistracted time with You, I am not going to get the refreshment I need to enter each day fully prepared.

I realize it's up to me to decide how high of a priority You are. It's so tempting to say, "If I can just get this done, then I'll spend time with God." But that never seems to work out. One distraction leads to the next...and the next. Prod me to be intentional about seeking You first. Only then will everything else fall into place so much better. The noise won't be as deafening, and I'll be more sensitive to Your nudges and whispers into my life.

Seek first the kingdom of God and His righteousness, and all these things shall be added to you.

MATTHEW 6:33

Prayer Wisdom

The Christian leader who seeks an example to follow does well to turn to the life of Jesus Himself. Our belief in the necessity of prayer comes from observing His life. Surely if anyone could have sustained life without prayer, it would be the very Son of God Himself…Prayer was the dominant feature of His life and a recurring part of His teaching. Prayer kept His moral vision sharp and clear. Prayer gave Him courage to endure the perfect but painful will of His Father. Prayer paved the way for transfiguration.[1]

J. OSWALD SANDERS

Prayer Is a Two-Way Street

Father, You gladly tell Your children to approach You with boldness and make our needs known. You ask us to place our burdens in Your hands, to bring our concerns to You. In the prayer that Jesus taught to the disciples, He included requests for daily bread and forgiveness. You are the source of all things, and to You I can come and ask for help and supply.

Yet I realize that prayer is also about listening—about letting You speak to my heart. When Jesus lifted up His model prayer, He first spoke with reverence for You in Your place of authority, then asked that Your will be done on earth as it is in heaven. When I pray, may I first acknowledge Your lordship over me, and examine whether I am doing Your will. For that to happen, I need to listen to You and Your Word. May I always remember that prayer is a two-way street and never take Your provision for granted.

Let us therefore come boldly to the throne of grace,
that we may obtain mercy and find grace
to help in time of need.

HEBREWS 4:16

A LIFELONG JOURNEY

Lord, when it comes to being a good leader, I realize I'm on a lifelong journey. The learning will never stop. Every day will bring new opportunities to grow wiser, sharpen old skills and build new ones, and serve as a better overseer of those who follow me.

With that in mind, may I always possess the spirit of a learner. May I be eager to ask questions and observe the example set by others. May I never be content with the way things are, and always look for ways to improve. May I maintain a humble spirit that is glad to receive the counsel and input of others.

May my zeal for learning never cease, for the more I grow, the better I can lead. And there's no greater place for me to learn than at Your feet, for You are the source of all perfect wisdom.

Be filled with the knowledge of His will
in all wisdom and spiritual understanding.

COLOSSIANS 1:9

Remembering God's Faithfulness

Lord, everything I have accomplished is because of You. As Psalm 139:16 says, "All the days ordained for me were written in your book before one of them came to be" (NIV). Before I was born, You set out Your plans for me. You have brought me to where I am, and You are the source of every good gift I enjoy now. As for my future, that has been determined and is secure in Your hands as well!

I cannot take credit for any of the blessings You have poured out upon me. I have much to be grateful for, and I admit I am frequently forgetful of that. Motivate me to make a habit of recounting—again and again—the many ways You have provided for me. As my memory is refreshed, so is my heart. You are a faithful God—great is Your faithfulness!

God is faithful, by whom you were called
into the fellowship of His Son.

1 CORINTHIANS 1:9

A Fountain of Blessings

Lord, thank You that every time I read the Bible, I am given a new supply of exactly what I need for daily life. There are so many ways I am nourished by Your Word. It is a perpetual fountain of blessings to me, a light for every step I take on the path of life.

Because of Your Word, I am filled with the courage I need when challenges arise. I have abundant wisdom for the decisions I must make. I am inspired to persevere when I am unsure whether I can take another step. And I am reminded that You are faithful and will sustain me no matter what happens.

Because of the riches Your Word offers to me, may I let it dwell richly within me. May I meditate upon it and engrave it upon my heart so that I will apply it to everything I do.

His delight is the law of the LORD,
And in His law he meditates day and night.
He shall be like a tree planted by rivers of water.

PSALM 1:2-3

Praying Wisely

Father, when Solomon became king, You said, "Ask! What shall I give you?" (1 Kings 3:5). You basically offered him a blank check. Solomon's response was surprisingly simple: He asked for wisdom, which pleased You. There were many things he could have requested yet didn't. And when the king answered, he did so with a humility that acknowledged his complete dependence upon You.

When I lift my prayers to You, Lord, may I pay careful attention to what I ask for. Does it line up with what You would want? Might a selfish motivation lurk behind any of my requests? Am I asking with a humble spirit? Will the results be of temporary value or eternal?

Cause me to weigh my prayers carefully as I bring them to You. As Jesus said in the Lord's Prayer, may I desire, above all, that Your will be done. May my heart be in sync with Yours when I seek Your provision.

You do not have because you do not ask.
You ask and do not receive, because you ask amiss,
that you may spend it on your pleasures.

JAMES 4:2-3

An Ever-Present Advisor

Father, You are the ultimate consultant, for You possess perfect wisdom. And You have gifted me with Your Holy Spirit, a counselor who lives within me and illuminates the teachings of Your Word so that I might know how You have called me to live.

When I need guidance, may I remember that You are an ever-present advisor. You are with me in my meetings, during my phone calls and email exchanges, and every time I am tasked with a decision to make. When it comes to seeking Your wisdom, You don't make it complicated. All I need to do is pray and ask: "If any of you lacks wisdom, let him ask of God, who gives to all liberally and without reproach, and it will be given to him" (James 1:5).

Thank You for giving so freely of Your counsel, which enables me to be a better leader.

Listen to counsel and receive instruction,
That you may be wise in your latter days.

PROVERBS 19:20

My Needs for Today

Father, when it comes to Your daily provisions, give me the discernment to avoid complacency in times of feast and discontentment in times of famine. When there is abundance and all is going well, I don't want to lose my motivation to give my best. And when times are difficult, I don't want discouragement to undermine my ability to lead well.

I am reminded of when You provided manna for the nation of Israel as the people traveled through the wilderness on their way to the Promised Land. You provided them with exactly what they needed each day—never too little, never too much.

May I trust Your provision for each day as it comes; You know my needs better than I do. And may I not let circumstances—whether good or bad—cause me to take my eyes off You. Because You are always faithful, I know it is possible for me to always be content.

> I have been young, and now am old;
> Yet I have not seen the righteous forsaken,
> Nor his descendants begging bread.

PSALM 37:25

Prayer Wisdom

Prayer is beyond any question the highest activity of the human soul. Man is at his greatest and highest when upon his knees he comes face to face with God.[2]

MARTYN LLOYD-JONES

My First Priority

Lord, as I consider the way You led the disciples during Your ministry on earth, I am struck by the fact You spent much time in prayer. You sought time alone with Your heavenly Father, pouring out Your heart and seeking that His will be done, not Yours.

As I look at my to-do list for today—and every day—may I recognize the urgency of making prayer my first priority. It's when I commune with You that I'm able to view my list through Your eyes and better determine how to plan my day. As I pray, remind me to ask: Am I seeking my will, or Yours? Am I depending on my wisdom, or Yours?

As I ponder the answers, help me to discern whether I am exercising self-centered or God-centered leadership. It's only as I pursue Your will that the results of my labors will please You.

O God, You are my God;
Early will I seek You.

PSALM 63:1

Taking Time to Be Grateful

Father, because leadership is so much about overseeing what's happening right now, it's easy for me to become all too focused on the "urgent needs of the moment" and overlook the many blessings You've already given me. In my earnestness to get things done, I've forgotten to thank You for what has been accomplished and the things that are going well.

In Philippians 4:6-7, You urge me to be anxious for nothing, and that my *every* prayer needs to be made with thanksgiving. Thank You for this reminder that You desire for me to live with a constant spirit of gratitude. And yes, I do have much to be grateful for, if I would just take the time to recount those blessings.

May I lift them up to You now—the people who do their jobs well, the goals achieved, the areas where progress has been made. Bring these to my mind so I can say thank You!

Let the peace of Christ rule in your hearts...
And be thankful.

COLOSSIANS 3:15 NIV

A LEADER'S MOST
IMPORTANT RESOURCE

Lord, I know all too well how important it is that I begin each day with prayer. As I connect with You, I am able to view my work through Your eyes and make sure I don't run ahead of You, but instead, walk alongside You and wait upon Your guidance.

I realize prayer is the most important resource I have for being a good leader. As I commune with You, I have Your wisdom, Your direction, and Your strength at my disposal. As I share my burdens with You, they become lighter. As I bring my needs before You, I know You'll faithfully provide. As I place my trust in You, my anxieties will decrease. As I ask for Your Spirit to lead me, I am able to bear the fruit of the Spirit.

That's what prayer makes available to me! May I be more resolved than ever to make it my starting point for each day.

Having risen a long while before daylight,
He went out and departed to a solitary place;
and there He prayed.

MARK 1:35

THE KEY TO SUCCESS

Lord, none of what I do as a leader will matter if I'm not living in full submission to Your Word. I am reminded of Your instructions to Joshua when he became a newly minted leader and was tasked with the monumental responsibility of leading Your people into the Promised Land: "This Book of the Law shall not depart from your mouth, but you shall meditate in it day and night, that you may observe to do according to all that is written in it. For then you will make your way prosperous, and then you will have good success" (Joshua 1:8).

You made a very direct connection between obeying Your Word and knowing true success. May I make a habit of turning to Scripture daily for inspiration, wisdom, and direction. May I treat it as my go-to manual for all that I do. I ask that You would give me frequent reminders that if I want to prosper as a leader, I must love and observe Your Word.

> May the LORD be with you; and may you prosper,
> and build the house of the LORD your God,
> as He has said to you. Only may the LORD
> give you wisdom and understanding...that
> you may keep the law of the LORD your God.

1 CHRONICLES 22:11-12

ENDING EACH DAY WITH PRAYER

Lord, as I end each day, I find myself already becoming preoccupied with all that awaits me the next day. Though tomorrow isn't here yet, I'm already depleting today's energy on it.

Yet Your Word wisely says, "Don't worry about tomorrow…Today's trouble is enough for today" (Matthew 6:34 NLT). Help me to take that to heart—to realize that You've got me covered for today, and You've got me covered for tomorrow as well. So as I wrap up each day, instead of losing sleep over the next, may I relax my mind by giving today's results to You and asking You to bless them. May I take to heart what I have accomplished so that I can rejoice in the fruit of my labors.

I can see the wisdom of not only beginning my days with prayer but ending them with prayer as well. Then I will truly rest during the time You've designed for me to rest.

I will both lie down in peace, and sleep;
For You alone, O LORD, make me dwell in safety.

PSALM 4:8

The Value of Rest

Father, in today's work ethic, productivity is everything. And with the never-ending responsibilities I face as a leader, the pressure is constant for me to get things done. So when downtime does come, I admit I find myself wanting to keep working—just so I can make progress.

Yet You created us not only to work, but to rest. From the very beginning You set the example. On the seventh day of creation week, You ceased from all labor. The fact You gave us bodies that wear out daily and need refreshing should be a powerful hint as well. Rest is necessary so that we can replenish ourselves spiritually, mentally, and physically.

Help me to see rest as an essential part of my schedule. With it, I am more able to give my best. Instead of seeing rest as cutting into my productivity, may I view it as contributing to my performance.

God blessed the seventh day and sanctified it,
because in it He rested from all His work
which God had created and made.

GENESIS 2:3

Reflecting on God's Goodness

Lord, You are an almighty God. As I look to the past, I am reminded of the many wonderful ways You have worked in my life. You have directed my path, provided for my needs, and brought me to where I am today. The evidence of Your faithfulness abounds!

I know there have also been times when You've acted on my behalf without me being aware of it. You've watched over me even when I've questioned Your presence. As Psalm 121:3 says, You are my keeper who never slumbers.

I am encouraged as I remember Your mighty deeds. Bring them to my mind frequently! And I know You have good plans for my future. I look forward to watching them unfold in the days ahead. I praise You for caring so much about me!

> Your steadfast love, O LORD, extends to the heavens,
> your faithfulness to the clouds.

PSALM 36:5 ESV

THE TREASURE OF TIME

Father, as I go from day to day, it's hard to perceive how quickly time goes by. Sometimes progress can seem so slow that it's hardly noticeable. And because of the many routine tasks I handle each day, it may appear as though not much is happening.

But every once in a great while I look back and realize just how quickly time has gone by! Then I am struck by how short life is. I find myself wishing I had used my time better or set certain goals earlier. I've allowed days to slip away without making the most of them.

James 4:14 awakens me to the truth that every single day counts: "What is your life? It is even a vapor that appears for a little time and then vanishes away." May I never take for granted even one hour You've given me. I want to be a good steward who truly values the treasure of time.

The grass withers,
And its flower falls away,
But the word of the LORD endures forever.

1 PETER 1:24-25

Prayer Wisdom

Although I'd heard that prayer would deepen my relationship with God, I had never experienced it. But when I started to spend regular, daily, unhurried time in prayer—when I lingered in intimate conversation with God, the most intimate communion we can have with Him—that deeper relationship was mine! When you and I commune in prayer with God and experience that deeper relationship, we grow spiritually in a multitude of ways.[3]

ELIZABETH GEORGE

THE TEACHABLE LEADER

Father, if there is one attitude that makes it possible for a good leader to become a great one, it is teachability. Unless I realize there is always room for me to improve upon my skills, I am bound to end up in a rut—and do a disservice to my workplace and the people who look to me for direction and input about their productivity.

I admit change doesn't always come easily for me. Learning takes time and effort. Making room for new growth can be challenging when I'm already overwhelmed by busyness. But if adapting means progress, it will also mean becoming a better leader.

Rather than settle for what is simply good, I want to eagerly pursue what is best. When new wisdom or resources become available, may I seek them out rather than resist them. If there is any barrier of pride within me, point it out so that I may replace it with a teachable spirit.

A wise man will hear and increase learning,
And a man of understanding will attain wise counsel.

PROVERBS 1:5

A Surrendered Vessel

Father, I am grateful for Your faithfulness. In the times when I fail, You remain steadfast at my side. When I neglect my relationship with You and ignore Your guidance, You keep Your promise that the work You began in me will continue until it is completed (Philippians 1:6). You are doing what is necessary to bring about the ultimate good You want in me even though I have yet to understand what is happening.

When I find myself falling short as a believer and a leader, convict me of my need to lean on You even more. It's when I yield myself to You and trust You that You're able to mold me. Make me soft clay in Your hands so that Your purpose will be done. I marvel at the paradox that when I am humble, You will lift me up (James 4:10). That's the kind of leader I want to be—a surrendered vessel You can work through.

I will praise You, O LORD, with my whole heart;
I will tell of all Your marvelous works.

PSALM 9:1

IN SEARCH OF WISDOM COMPANIONS

Lord, Your Word says that "in the multitude of counselors there is safety" (Proverbs 11:14). Thank You for this reminder of the value of surrounding myself with other believers who can encourage and challenge me in both my spiritual growth and my role as a leader.

I pray that I would be deliberate about building relationships with peers and role models whom I can look to for wisdom and insight. I know I can benefit from ongoing interaction with others who will have a positive influence on me. As You have said so perfectly, "Iron sharpens iron" (Proverbs 27:17).

When I get together with my wisdom companions, may I have the humility of a good listener, the attitude of a learner, and the diligence to apply the counsel I receive. May I also show gratitude for the ways these friends invest in my life. And when opportunities arise for me to return the favor, may I be quick to make myself available.

Without counsel, plans go awry,
But in the multitude of counselors they are established.

PROVERBS 15:22

Each Day a Fresh Start

Father, I am filled with anticipation for this new day. I love how each morning comes with a natural infusion of optimism and hope. Thank You for granting me—once again—a fresh opportunity to plan ahead, determine my priorities, use my time well, make the most of each task, and be a positive influence on every person I encounter.

Before I begin in earnest, I want to sit quietly at Your feet and listen to the promptings You place on my heart. My desire is to walk in step with You as the day unfolds.

Today is a gift from You; may I make every moment, every hour count. And when the day ends, may I bring the results back to You as an offering of thanks and ask for Your blessings on my labors. Then when I awake the next morning, may my enthusiasm for what is to come begin anew!

> I rise before the dawning of the morning,
> And cry for help;
> I hope in Your word.

PSALM 119:147

GOD'S GIFT OF TOTAL ACCESS

Father, I *know* how vital prayer is for me. It connects me with You and helps me to reset myself according to Your desires. Yet still I struggle with so many temptations not to pray: I'm too busy. I feel as though I don't deserve to come into Your presence. I question why a certain prayer hasn't been answered yet. I feel as though I'm not spiritual enough. I've failed at a specific temptation repeatedly and am unworthy. I'm not eloquent enough—it's hard for me to find the right words.

Help me to recognize these kinds of thoughts are from the enemy, who does not want me to pray! Because of all that You've entrusted to me as a leader, I cannot afford to skip time alone with You. When I am tempted, remind me that prayer is a 24/7 lifeline. I can't live or lead without it. Prayer is Your gift of total access to You; I want to use this gift well.

The LORD will command His
lovingkindness in the daytime,
And in the night His song shall be with me—
A prayer to the God of my life.

PSALM 42:8

What Can I Learn Today?

Lord, what can I learn today from the people whom I lead? I realize that just because my job title puts me in a position of authority over them doesn't mean they have nothing to offer to me. You have gifted every person around me in special ways so that we can all gain from our interactions with one another.

In Scripture, You talk about how every part of the church, the body of Christ, needs the other parts (1 Corinthians 12:12-26). And even if my workplace isn't the church, the principle still applies: As fellow staffers we all work toward common goals. Every one of us is needed to get the job done.

So may I look to my interactions with others as opportunities to learn, to grow, to be enriched personally. Teach me to lead in ways that let others shine so we can enjoy mutually beneficial working relationships. Make me a leader who not only gives but gladly receives new insights.

Let us consider one another
in order to stir up love and good works.

HEBREWS 10:24

THE BIBLE, MY GUIDE

Lord, when I open the pages of the Bible, I am meeting with You. I am opening myself to Your counsel and guidance not only for today but all my days.

As I read, fill my mind with your wisdom and truth. Speak what I need to hear. Lead me so that I, in turn, will know how to lead others. Psalm 1 tells me that as I meditate on Your Word day and night, I will become like a tree planted by the rivers of water, bearing lush leaves and bringing forth fruit (verses 2-3). I want to be that kind of tree! As I allow Your truth to take root in me, I'll know how it is You want me to live—and to lead.

As I receive Your Word, may I be determined to do whatever it takes to engrave it upon my heart so I don't forget Your instructions.

The testimony of the LORD is sure,
making wise the simple.

PSALM 19:7

Prayer Wisdom

Be sure to set the presence of God before you in prayer; have a real sight of the infinite greatness, majesty, and glory of that you are presenting yourself to when you are calling upon him. If you have a real sight of God in his glory, it will keep your heart close to the duty of prayer…if you would present the Lord in his glory and greatness, excellency, majesty, and power before you, and what a dreadful God he is in himself, and yet what a merciful God he is to us in his Son, this will mightily compose your heart.[4]

JEREMIAH BURROUGHS

GROWING AS A LEADER

Father, I don't want to be a stagnant leader, one who isn't growing. I want to challenge myself to get better at what I do. One way to do that is to strive each day to reflect You more and more in my life. In becoming more like You, I'll also grow as a leader.

Second Corinthians 3:18 says that as I behold You and Your glory, I will be transformed more into Your image. Romans 8:29 says Your plan for me is to become more like Your Son, Jesus. To pursue Christlikeness, then, is to pursue growth—the kind that will make me a better leader.

As I read the pages of Scripture, open my eyes to the ways in which You lead. Every one of Your attributes offers leadership lessons—alert me to what I need to learn. Thank You for giving me Your Word as "a lamp to my feet and a light to my path" (Psalm 119:105).

Him we preach...teaching every man in all wisdom, that we may present every man perfect in Christ Jesus.

COLOSSIANS 1:28-29

GOD'S INFINITE STRENGTH

Father, I rejoice in Your greatness! As I look at all of creation, I see Your might on display. From the deepest seas to the highest mountains, and to the outermost reaches of space and beyond, Your power is manifest. You established all the laws of nature; You keep all the planets and stars on their paths. You control and sustain all order in the universe—a testimony to Your infinite strength.

This brings all the more meaning to Isaiah 41:10, where You say, "I am your God. I will strengthen you, Yes, I will help you, I will uphold you with My righteous right hand." I am overwhelmed as I consider that I have access to the very same power that created and controls the universe. It doesn't make sense for me to try to do things in my own strength, does it?

You make it possible for me to do great things because You are a great God. Strengthen me for all that You have called me to do!

O LORD, how manifold are Your works!
In wisdom You have made them all.

PSALM 104:24

My Cultivation as a Leader   39

CONTROLLED BY THE SPIRIT

Father, when a serious problem arose in the early church and leaders were needed to find a solution, the top requirement set by the apostles was that these leaders be "full of the Holy Spirit" (Acts 6:3). Being Spirit-led was ranked before human ability.

While the context in Acts 6 is the church, even so, I can see how in secular workplaces a leader controlled by the Spirit will lead differently than one who isn't. A leader who is indwelt by the Spirit has a "Helper" (John 16:7); a "guide...into all truth" (verse 13); can bear "the fruit of the Spirit" (Galatians 5:22-23); is made more like Christ (2 Corinthians 3:18); and possesses a source of love (Romans 5:5), hope (15:13), and wisdom (Colossians 1:9).

So whether I work in a church or nonchurch setting, may I begin each day by fully yielding myself to Your Spirit. In this way I will become a leader who is filled with the Spirit, able to accomplish what I could never do without Him.

Be filled with the Spirit.

EPHESIANS 5:18

PRAYING FOR MY COWORKERS

Lord, I want to be a leader who thoughtfully and deliberately prays for my coworkers. May I seek to be informed of their needs and circumstances so I can pray with wisdom for them.

In Scripture, I read of how Your Spirit intercedes for me in prayer, and how the apostle Paul prayed on behalf of others. Daniel prayed for the nation of Israel, as did Your prophets.

Thank You for the way that intercessory prayer will increase my love for my coworkers and give me new opportunities to see You at work in their lives. And as the answers come, I will also have the privilege of rejoicing alongside them.

When my prayers become too self-focused, burden my heart with the desire to pray for those around me. Expand my prayer horizons so that I may see Your provision in more ways than ever.

I exhort first of all that supplications, prayers, intercessions, and giving of thanks be made for all men.

1 TIMOTHY 2:1

Always Learning

Lord, it is said the best leaders are those who are always learning. I realize there's no better way to grow in wisdom and insight than by reading Your Word, which "is profitable for doctrine, for reproof, for correction, for instruction in righteousness, that the man of God may be complete, thoroughly equipped for every good work" (2 Timothy 3:16-17).

I desire to be that leader who is thoroughly equipped for every good work. Instill within me a hunger that feeds upon Your Scriptures daily. As I read, may I carefully ponder Your instructions so they guide my thinking and actions. Romans 15:4 says "everything that was written in the past was written to teach us" (NIV). As I look to the examples of leaders who loved and followed You, may I eagerly apply their lessons to my own life. As I take Your Word to heart, mold me into the kind of leader You want me to be.

All these things happened to them as examples,
and they were written for our admonishment.

1 CORINTHIANS 10:11

PRAYER WISDOM

The key to praying with power is to become the kind of persons who do not use God for our ends but are utterly devoted to being used for his ends.[5]

JOHN PIPER

When the Past Haunts Me

Father, when past mistakes come back to haunt me, remind me to release the pain into Your hands. I don't want to succumb to the temptations to pity myself or to let my regrets hinder me from moving forward. Replace my negative thoughts with positive memories of the good You have done in my life after bad things have happened.

I recognize there is nothing I can do about what's past. And I know You are a compassionate God who hears my prayers and holds out a helping hand. When I feel unworthy to approach You, fill my mind with the many assurances in Scripture that Your love for me is steadfast and unshakeable.

I ask that You would lift me up and fill me with a resolve to see today as an opportunity for a fresh start. The slate is blank, and with You at my side, I can fill it with good things that give me reasons to rejoice.

You observe trouble and grief,
To repay it by Your hand.
The helpless commits himself to You.

PSALM 10:14

GROWING IN THE
PRACTICE OF PRAYER

Lord, as a Christian, prayer should be as natural to me as breathing. Within me is a longing to walk closer to You, yet I don't always follow up on that by taking time to pray. You've given this gift so I can talk with You, and I can't think of a better way to show my love for You than by spending time alone with You.

When I do pray, sometimes I find myself falling into the rut of repetition or becoming easily distracted. Then I become discouraged, thinking I don't have what it takes to make this a fruitful discipline. That's when I need Your reminder that prayer is as simple as opening my heart to You, and that persistence is the answer when I'm tempted to give up. The best way to pray well is to keep praying.

Because Your Spirit dwells in me, I have a helper who enables me. In the Spirit's power, I *can* grow in the practice of prayer. Thank You for this wonderful gift, Lord!

Pray without ceasing.

1 THESSALONIANS 5:17

My Cultivation as a Leader

PART 2

MY CALLING AS A LEADER

OPEN MY EYES, LORD

Lord, help me to view every person under my leader-ship through Your eyes. Everyone who works along-side me does so by Your divine appointment and has been brought into my life for a purpose.

I confess that some people are easier to work with than others. And I admit I get frustrated with those who are "high maintenance." Yet I know Your calling for me is not to show favoritism, but as much as is pos-sible, to live in harmony and at peace with everyone (Romans 12:18).

Help me to make a genuine effort to build good relationships with each person You have placed around me. May I value my coworkers not only for the tasks they do, but as individuals who were created by You and are loved by You. Open my eyes to what makes each one special and alert me to opportunities for affirming them. Shape my perspective so that the way in which I lead encourages and builds up everyone.

> Let us pursue the things which make for peace
> and the things by which one may edify another.
>
> **ROMANS 14:19**

GOD'S NEVER-ENDING GRACE

Heavenly Father, You get all the credit for bringing me to the place where I am today. It is by Your grace that You have gifted me with the skills and responsibilities I possess. At the times when I wanted to give up, You sustained me. Everything I have achieved is due to Your generosity in my life.

May I never take for granted Your faithfulness to me. When things go wrong or I get discouraged, remind me of the many ways You have helped me in the past. May I do as the psalmist did and "remember your miracles of long ago...and meditate on all your mighty deeds" (Psalm 77:11-12 NIV).

As I carry out my plans for the future, I want to include You in them. It's so easy to become prideful and do things in my own strength. When that happens, I am certain to fail. You are my everything, Lord. Thank You for Your never-ending grace.

> God is able to make all grace abound toward you,
> that you, always having all sufficiency in all things,
> may have an abundance for every good work.

2 CORINTHIANS 9:8

Getting Along with My Fellow Leaders

Lord, I realize that good leadership doesn't happen in a vacuum. It requires that I work with my fellow leaders. And I realize we won't always be in agreement about the decisions we need to make as we lead together.

In Your Word, You say that "many advisors bring success" (Proverbs 15:22 NLT). You tell us, "Do nothing out of selfish ambition or vain conceit. Rather, in humility value others above yourselves, not looking to your own interests but each of you to the interests of the others" (Philippians 2:3-4 NIV). You urge us to "live at peace with everyone" (Romans 12:18 NIV).

This means being a leader who listens and considers all the options. It means working with others in ways that builds them up rather than tears them down. May I be a positive contributor when I work with my fellow leaders so that they may see You clearly in my words and actions.

Pursue peace with all people.

HEBREWS 12:14

How Well Am I Doing?

Lord, as I consider how people respond to my leadership, may I realize that ultimately, You are the best judge of how well I am doing. While feedback from those around me can be helpful, still, I have to ask: What do *You* think? How am I doing according to what *You* expect of me?

You alone know the true state of my heart. Open my eyes to the times when I slip to becoming a people-pleaser, cutting corners to achieve a goal, or doing things in the hopes of getting something favorable in return. As Your Word says, may I do my service "as to the Lord, and not to men" (Ephesians 6:7). May I live with the constant awareness that one day, I will stand before You and give an account for the kind of leader I was.

My desire is to truly honor You in all that I do. As I lead, may I do so with the goal of pleasing You.

> It is a very small thing that I should be
> judged by you or by a human court...
> but He who judges me is the Lord.
>
> **1 CORINTHIANS 4:3-4**

NOT JUST ANOTHER DAY

Lord, as one day flows into the next, and yet again the next, it's easy to forget how each one is a new opportunity to give my best to every task I do and every person I meet. Just because my days are filled with repetitious routines doesn't mean I have to be lulled into complacency, or to view anyone or anything as merely ordinary.

Help me to remember that Your presence in my life is what makes every day special. Your Word wonderfully proclaims that Your "compassions…are new every morning" (Lamentations 3:22-23). And I can live with the confidence that "in the morning…you hear my voice" (Psalm 5:3 NIV). That's true every single day!

Impress on my heart the truth that each time I wake up comes with a fresh opportunity to ask for new measures of Your compassion, wisdom, guidance, and strength—as well as new chances to grow, expand my horizons, strengthen my relationships, and pursue my dreams.

Satisfy us in the morning with your steadfast love,
that we may rejoice and be glad all our days.

PSALM 90:14 ESV

ACCORDING TO GOD'S PLAN

Lord, I recognize that You have placed me where I am today. I am not here by accident. You orchestrated my past and opened the doors that led to what I am doing right now. In Your Word, You say that whatever You plan *will* come to pass.

May the awareness of Your past designs over my life give me a confidence that Your plans will carry me into the future. When I place myself in Your hands, I have nothing to worry about. My days have already been determined on Your calendar, and You have promised You will never forsake me.

Thank You, Father, for Your ongoing care of me, a care that will continue through all of my days. May I never cease to thank You and credit You for what I have accomplished.

The steps of a good man are ordered by the LORD,
And He delights in his way.

PSALM 37:23

PRAYER WISDOM

The beloved apostle John summed up perhaps the most important prayer-principle of all when he wrote, "Now this is the confidence that we have in Him, that if we ask *anything according to His will*, He hears us. And if we know that He hears us, whatever we ask, we know that we have the petitions that we have asked of Him" (1 John 5:14-15). When our desires and requests are first aligned with and subjugated to the will of God, we know that He will hear and grant what we seek of Him.

How do we align our praying with the will of God? By getting to know the Scriptures. This is where God's will is revealed. Let the truth of Scripture shape your thinking and feed your appetites, and then you will know how to pray according to the will of God.[6]

JOHN MACARTHUR

A Serious Calling

Lord, as time passes and I spend day after day meeting obligations and deadlines, it's all too easy to let my responsibilities as a leader become routine. Yet there is nothing routine about good leadership; the calling You have given me should never be taken lightly.

Before I was born, You lovingly prepared the plans that would determine the direction of my life. You've placed people on my path who have poured themselves into me and made me what I am. Above all, You've guided my every step. May I never take for granted all that has been required to bring me to where I am today.

You've given me a serious calling—may I be equally serious about how I fulfill it. Each day as I wake up, may I look to my responsibilities with a renewed vigor to give my best to all that I do, no matter how routine it may seem.

> Whatever you do, work at it with all your heart,
> as working for the Lord, not human masters.

COLOSSIANS 3:23 NIV

THE KIND OF LEADERSHIP GOD BLESSES

Lord, the more I seek Your wisdom, the more opportunity I am given to become conformed to Your image. That which I behold, I will become. The more I focus on You and Your Word, the more I am enabled to walk in Your footsteps and imitate You.

My heart's desire is to be a distinctly Christian leader and to reflect Your leadership qualities in all I do. As I consider the abundance of how-to resources on ways to become a better leader, please gift me with the discernment to seek out those leadership principles that are in line with Your teaching and Your example. Equip me to recognize and apply the guidelines and practices that are consistent with Your Word, and to set aside those that aren't.

This is the kind of leader I want to be, Lord, for I know this is the kind of leadership You will bless.

We all, with unveiled face, beholding as in a mirror
the glory of the Lord, are being transformed
into the same image from glory to glory.

2 CORINTHIANS 3:18

LEADING WITH LOVE

Lord, You are the most loving leader who has ever walked the earth. First John 4:8 proclaims, "God is love." And that love radiates brilliantly from the first page of Scripture to the last. You also call us to imitate Your love and show it to one another.

As I consider the way I lead, may I measure myself according to 1 Corinthians 13:4-8: "Love is patient, love is kind. It does not envy, it does not boast, it is not proud. It does not dishonor others, it is not self-seeking, it is not easily angered, it keeps no record of wrongs. Love does not delight in evil but rejoices with the truth. It always protects, always trusts, always hopes, always perseveres" (NIV).

May all those characteristics of love be true about my leadership. I know I won't always get it right—but as I walk in the Spirit, I am enabled to bear the fruit of the Spirit, which includes love. Thank You for empowering me!

> Everyone who loves is born of God
> and knows God. He who does not love
> does not know God, for God is love.
>
> **1 JOHN 4:7-8**

Leading from Above
or Alongside?

Lord, one lesson You made very clear during Your time of ministry on earth is that being a leader requires a shepherd's heart. At the same time that You led and taught Your disciples, You cared for them. Everything You did while leading them was prompted out of genuine concern and love. You were protective and did not back away from doing what was right and necessary for their well-being.

As I ask, "What kind of leader am I?," I realize I could just as well ask, "What kind of shepherd am I?" Do I tend to lead from above, or do I come alongside? Are my words and actions designed to bring benefit to myself, or to others? Am I so focused on what I need to get done that I'm not truly caring about those who are under my charge?

Help me to cultivate a shepherd's mindset, Lord, so that I can lead more effectively.

> Let each of us please his neighbor
> for his good, to build him up.

ROMANS 15:2 ESV

Living Leadership

Lord, yet another way that You demonstrated great leadership is by living out what You taught. You led by example. You didn't just do the talk; You also did the walk. Your followers were in a living lab; Your words came to life through Your actions.

You didn't seclude Yourself behind a closed door or a large desk. You didn't merely bark out assignments then expect people to figure out the applications on their own. You were available, You listened, You answered questions, and You turned Your precepts into real-life experiences. You lived out Your leadership to the extent people could know real and permanent change.

May Your example inspire me to stretch my boundaries as a leader. May I never tire of learning from Your example of a vibrant, interactive leadership!

> He shepherded them according to
> the integrity of his heart,
> And guided them by
> the skillfulness of his hands.
>
> **PSALM 78:72**

The One Main Goal

Lord, Hebrews 12:2 says that for the joy set before You, You endured the cross. Though You greatly dreaded the excruciating pain to come, You kept Your eyes on the ultimate goal: to bring glory to Your heavenly Father by saving the lost and restoring them back to You.

Everything You did during Your earthly ministry kept that final objective in mind. Yes, You took care of people's needs of the moment, but You always did so with the ultimate need in view. In some way or other, Your every word and action pointed to Your one mission, Your one purpose: to bring glory to the Father. In today's language, we would say You were focused.

As I lead, may I be equally fervent. May I consider how each day's goals can contribute toward the one main goal of my life. Help me to overcome the tendency to think small, within the confines of each day, and instead, think big, with a dedicated focus on bringing honor to God.

Whatever you do, do all to the glory of God.

1 CORINTHIANS 10:31

The Necessity of Hard Work

Lord, I realize that even if I am the greatest visionary in the world, unless I am willing to do the hard work of putting my desires into action, my visions will remain nothing more than empty dreams.

This means rolling up my sleeves, considering all the options, planning a course of action, and carrying it out. Very simply, turning a vision into reality takes work. I realize that without effort, there can be no reward.

Thank You for Scripture's reminder that I am to "run in such a way as to get the prize" (1 Corinthians 9:24 NIV). Many steps are required before I can reach the finish line. And much preparation is necessary even before I start the race. Help me to plan well and run well so that I may finish well.

> Do you see a man who excels in his work?
> He will stand before kings;
> He will not stand before unknown men.

PROVERBS 22:29

PRAYER WISDOM

The Christian should work as if all depended on him, and pray as if all depended on God.[7]

C.H. SPURGEON

PURSUING GOD'S KIND OF SUCCESS

Lord, in today's world, success is measured by job titles, material well-being, and achievements. Yet I recognize it is possible to be accomplished in all these but fail miserably when it comes to what really counts.

As I determine my priorities and goals, equip me to discern between the temporary and the eternal, the things of earth versus the things of heaven, and whether I am seeking people-approval instead of God-approval. Which am I going to choose? Am I more concerned about being successful according to the world's measure, or Yours?

Open my eyes afresh to what true success is all about from Your perspective. As Matthew 6:33 says, may I seek Your kingdom first before all else. Only then will I know the kind of success that is real and lasting.

Do not lay up for yourselves treasures on earth,
where moth and rust destroy and where thieves
break in and steal; but lay up for yourselves
treasures in heaven, where neither moth nor rust
destroys and where thieves do not break in and steal.
For where your treasure is, there your heart will be also.

MATTHEW 6:19-21

A Focus on Blessing Others

Father, as I connect with people today, may I make a thoughtful and deliberate effort to be a blessing to them. May I think not in terms of what I can gain, but what I can give. In every interaction, help me to be ready with my full attention and my heart.

May I "do nothing out of selfish ambition or vain conceit," but rather, "in humility value others" above me (Philippians 2:3 NIV). Give me the wisdom to recognize the ways I can encourage and lift others up—so that through me, they can see the same kind of care You show to everyone who seeks and follows You.

At every opportunity given to me, Lord, teach me how I can be others-focused in what I say and do. I want to be a good steward of the work relationships You have entrusted to me.

Each of you should use whatever gift you have received to serve others, as faithful stewards of God's grace.

1 PETER 4:10 NIV

A Next-Generation Leader

Father, Your Son is the supreme example of a next-generation leader. He poured Himself into the Twelve, and the results speak for themselves worldwide! I too want to be a next-generation leader—one who equips, encourages, and prays for those who will one day fill my shoes. Inspire me with a vision for raising up people who can blaze new trails and reach new heights.

To do this requires being a leader who is both available and a role model that others can follow. May I commit to being the kind of leader people want to imitate. Even though I am in the role of overseer, I recognize I am also accountable to those I am training. Give me the sensitivity to know when to entrust them with new and greater responsibilities and step out of the way of their growth.

Enable me with the wisdom to figure out how to lead by example so that new leaders may rise up and do their jobs well.

Show yourself in all respects
to be a model of good works, and
in your teaching show integrity,
dignity, and sound speech.

TITUS 2:7-8 ESV

ABIDING IN THE LORD

Father, I am weary. So much is going on, and I'm feeling overwhelmed. When that happens, my first inclination is to try harder. To muster up more strength. To call upon what's left of my energy reserves and wear myself out even more.

Yet You have said that apart from You, I cannot do anything (John 15:5). It's only when I abide in You—when I pursue an active relationship with You and place my complete dependence upon You—that I can be filled with your kind of strength and endure. You have promised that "those who wait on the LORD shall renew their strength; they shall mount up with wings like eagles, they shall run and not be weary, they shall walk and not faint" (Isaiah 40:31).

May I abide in You at all times so that I am living in Your power and not my own. Thank You for providing me with exactly what I need to get through each hour and each day.

Abide in Me, and I in you.
As the branch cannot bear fruit of itself,
unless it abides in the vine, neither can you,
unless you abide in Me.

JOHN 15:4

GOD LOOKS AT THE HEART

Father, as I survey the qualifications You list in Scripture for selecting leaders, I notice that above all, You call for spiritual maturity and moral integrity. Rather than look at a person's skill set, You look at the heart.

As I evaluate how I'm doing as a leader, help me to pay attention to the qualities You desire most—including a love for Your Word, a humble spirit, and a heart fully yielded to You. When Joshua replaced Moses as leader over all Israel, You promised that obedience to Your Word would bring success (Joshua 1:8). You were pleased with King David because he was a man after Your heart (Acts 13:22). You lifted up King Solomon because he sought wisdom instead of riches (1 Kings 3:7-14). First Peter 5:6 says You exalt the humble.

For You, Lord, when it comes to leadership, it is the inner person that counts. May I pursue the qualities You seek.

The LORD does not see as man sees;
for man looks at the outward appearance,
but the LORD looks at the heart.

1 SAMUEL 16:7

A Mark of Real Love

Lord, help me to realize that my capacity to love is best measured by my willingness to forgive. You have demonstrated that real love comes with forgiveness—that's what You showed to a hostile, evil crowd that nailed Your Son to the cross.

To say I am loving means being able to say I am also forgiving—and You made it clear how far our love should extend by urging us to love even our enemies (Matthew 5:44). When asked how often we should forgive, You said "seventy times seven" (Matthew 18:21-22). That was Your way of saying, "Keep on forgiving."

You forgive so generously that Your mercies are new every morning. May I enter each day with a readiness to forgive. In doing this I show my gratitude for Your forgiveness, and I enable others to see You through me.

Be kind to one another, tenderhearted,
forgiving one another, even as
God in Christ forgave you.

EPHESIANS 4:32

Prayer Wisdom

What is prayer? It is the communion of the spiritual life in the soul of man with its Divine Author; it is a breathing back the Divine life into the bosom of God from whence it came; it is holy, spiritual converse with God…It is a talking with God as a child talks with his father, as a friend converses with his friend…true prayer is the aspiration of a renewed soul towards God: it is the breathing of the Divine life, sometimes in the accents of sorrow, sometimes as the expression of want, and always as the acknowledgment of dependence; it is the looking up of a renewed, afflicted, necessitous, and dependent child to its own loving Father.[8]

OCTAVIUS WINSLOW

BRINGING HONOR TO THE LORD

Lord, as I read 1 Corinthians 10:31, I am reminded there is a higher purpose behind all my work: "Whatever you do, do all to the glory of God." Can I honestly say that everything I do is done in a way that brings honor to You—even the seemingly mundane tasks?

To answer that question, I need to set aside time for self-examination. Are my words and actions consistent with what You want of me? Are they marked by integrity, truthfulness, humility, and love? Am I intentional about seeking what is best for others? Would the way I exercise my leadership receive Your stamp of approval? And most important of all, in what areas do I need to improve?

Show me, Lord, where I have room to grow. I really do want to bring honor to You in all things great and small.

Whatever you do in word or deed,
do all in the name of the Lord Jesus, giving
thanks to God the Father through Him.

COLOSSIANS 3:17

BEARING ANOTHER
LEADER'S BURDENS

Father, You ask us to bear one another's burdens (Galatians 6:2). Today I want to pray for my brothers and sisters in Christ who are in leadership positions and facing serious difficulties right now.

I lift up those who are in government positions and facing political peer pressure to compromise their biblical convictions. I ask Your protection and provision for those who serve in countries where Christians are persecuted or people are seriously impoverished. I ask Your help as well for those leaders who work in strongly anti-Christian environments—that they not become discouraged, but that they endure and receive Your blessing for standing as ambassadors who shine Your light into a dark world.

Thank You for caring for these leaders. I know that You have strategically placed them where they are so that Your work can be accomplished. And if there are tangible ways I can help them, may I do so quickly and generously.

Pray in the Spirit on all occasions with all kinds of prayers and requests. With this in mind, be alert and always keep on praying for all the Lord's people.

EPHESIANS 6:18 NIV

THE NEED TO DELEGATE

Father, one of my ongoing struggles is a tendency to take on more work than I can handle. I'm not always a good judge of what I should do myself and what I should delegate to others. The result is predictable: I end up wearing myself out, and some tasks don't get done as well as they should. Help me to recognize what I do best, set my priorities accordingly, and be willing to trust others with responsibilities that fit their skill set better or allow them to grow.

As a leader, I'm not called to play all the musical instruments. Rather, I am more like the conductor who coordinates all the individual musicians to create a harmonious result.

When I take on more than I should, convict me with the reminder that good leadership means knowing how to delegate. Help me to make the best use of people's talents so they can shine in their area of giftedness. You've made all of us different for a reason!

...from whom the whole body, joined and knit together by what every joint supplies, according to the effective working by which every part does its share.

EPHESIANS 4:16

TREASURES IN HEAVEN

Lord, though my job is such a big part of my life, help me to keep it in perspective compared to what is truly important.

Your Word calls me not to store up treasures for myself on earth, but in heaven (Matthew 6:19-20). So much of life is filled with things that are insignificant and won't last. I have to ask myself: How much energy am I devoting to pursuits that have no enduring value? What can I do now that will offer spiritual benefits I can enjoy for all eternity?

Equip me to look at my life through Your eyes. Help me to examine what I do and why. How can I use my skills, time, and possessions to bring greater honor to You and impart Your blessings to others? May I take greater delight in finding ways to use my job—and all the other areas of my life—to build up treasures in heaven.

Set your mind on things above,
not on things on the earth.

COLOSSIANS 3:2

BEING A RELATIONAL LEADER

Father, as a leader, I want to be a good steward of not just my work, but the people I work with. After all, if we're doing our jobs but not relating to each other well, that will affect everyone's performance. In the times when I become preoccupied with the end results, remind me of the need to put people first—to show that they're important to me.

That means going the extra mile and taking time to get to know and interact with them. I admit there are some persons I don't relate to as well as others. But I still want them to know that I care, that I appreciate them for their part in what we do.

Can I ask You to help me in this area? In the ways I fall short, give me ideas for how I can do better. Impress on my mind the principle that better relationships result in better work.

Let each of you look out not only for his own interests,
but also for the interests of others.

PHILIPPIANS 2:4

NOT PERFECTION, BUT FAITHFULNESS

Father, as I carry out my leadership responsibilities, may everything I do be consistent with Your calling for me as a believer. I don't want to bring shame to You. May I remain steadfast in my devotion to You so that I am also steadfast in doing my work in ways that honor You.

In Scripture, You compare the diligent Christian to an athlete who competes according to the rules, a soldier who endures hardship and seeks to please his commander, and a steward who guards the treasure of truth well (2 Timothy 2:3-5; 1:14).

I realize You aren't asking for perfection, but faithfulness. It's when I offer myself willingly to You that You are able to work through me as You wish. And in the times when I stumble and fall, I am grateful You are a God of grace—a heavenly Father who delights in forgiving and restoring me. May I lean upon Your enablement of me every step of the way.

The eyes of the LORD run to and fro
throughout the whole earth, to show Himself strong
on behalf of those whose heart is loyal to Him.

2 CHRONICLES 16:9

Giving Others a Sense of Purpose

Father, I know how meaningful it is for me to have a sense of purpose in what I do. That's what helps motivate me and give me focus.

As a leader, then, give me a sensitivity to the need other people have for a sense of purpose as well. When it comes to those who are under my charge, may I be deliberate in affirming what makes them unique, valuable, and an appreciated contributor. Though doing this will require careful thinking on my part, I know it will be time well invested—because a settled sense of purpose brings with it greater confidence and drive.

Give me the right words to say to bring encouragement to a person's heart. Rather than merely flatter, may my praise be heartfelt and fitting. I want to be a catalyst that enables others to get a clearer vision for how special they are.

Comfort each other and edify one another.

1 THESSALONIANS 5:11

Prayer Wisdom

All true prayer must be offered in full submission to God. After we have made our requests known to Him, our language should be, "Thy will be done." I would a thousand times rather that God's will should be done than my own. I cannot see the future as God can; therefore, it is a good deal better to let Him choose for me than to choose for myself.[9]

D.L. MOODY

WHAT REALLY COUNTS IN GOD'S EYES

Lord, thank You for the way Scripture gives me an eternal perspective on both life and leadership. I have found Jeremiah 9:23-24 very eye-opening: "Let not the wise man glory in his wisdom, let not the mighty man glory in his might, nor let the rich man glory in his riches; but let him who glories glory in this, that he understands and knows Me."

I am humbled as I read those words. I myself have fallen prey to the world's measurements for success. I have my own "trophies" that I cling to, achievements that give me stature and proclaim my qualifications to lead. Yet here, through the prophet Jeremiah, You remind me those are nothing in comparison to understanding and knowing You. That's what You prize. That's what really counts because that is what will last for eternity.

Thank You for teaching me to hold my successes very loosely, and instead, to prize an ever-deepening relationship with You.

When pride comes, then comes shame;
But with the humble is wisdom.

PROVERBS 11:2

SETTING THE RIGHT PACE

Lord, as I lead, give me the discernment to know the pace I should set for others. I don't want to run so far ahead that people become frustrated or discouraged. Give me the sensitivity to stay within their reach and put the finish line where it is attainable. Help me to strike the right balance between making workplace progress and setting objectives my coworkers can achieve.

I realize this means mastering the art of flexibility—of being willing to adjust plans, expectations, and goals in ways that keep others motivated and doesn't exhaust them. It also means practicing patience—a virtue I admit isn't always easy for me to exercise. Yet if I succumb to impatience, I'll end up being ineffective, failing to connect with people when they need it most.

Help me, Lord, to stay carefully in tune with each person's drive and ability so that I can maximize their sense of accomplishment.

Can two walk together, unless they are agreed?

AMOS 3:3

The Leader as Diplomat

Father, it seems as though much of my time is spent figuring out how to resolve delicate situations between two or more people. Differences of opinion have been voiced, and those involved have opposing convictions. How can I reconcile them without offending anyone or compromising any principles that might be at stake?

It's at times like these I especially need Your wisdom. As I attempt to negotiate the issues at hand, help me to respect the individuals involved, set aside my personal preferences, and effectively seek possible solutions. Enable me to figure out how I can cultivate a positive spirit that encourages everyone to be fair and offer their input for how we can achieve harmony. As they are given opportunity to find answers, they're given ownership of the solution.

Thank You that I don't need to walk this path alone. With Your help, and by nurturing cooperation, points of agreement can be found. Help me to master this art of diplomacy!

A soft answer turns away wrath,
But a harsh word stirs up anger.

PROVERBS 15:1

THE POWER OF INSPIRATION

Lord, I admire Nehemiah's leadership. The captives who had returned from Babylon to Jerusalem were in deep distress because their city and its walls lay in ruins. Nehemiah inspired them to action with a vision of what could happen if they all worked together—and in quick time, they "built the wall…for the people had a mind to work" (Nehemiah 4:6).

I see in this example the power of inspiration. Nehemiah had zeal and a vision—this stirred the people. Nehemiah's passion became theirs.

Do I have a genuine zeal for what I'm doing? And for the goals of our workplace? Do I communicate—in clear, simple ways—the benefits of our labors? Can I honestly say I have an enthusiasm that is contagious? And most important of all, am I walking closely with You as Nehemiah did? As I seek to inspire, I want to do so with You as my guide.

I told them of the hand of my God which had been good upon me, and also of the king's words that he had spoken to me. So they said, "Let us rise up and build." Then they set their hands to this good work.

NEHEMIAH 2:18

GREAT LEADERS ARE
GREAT IN PRAYER

Father, one trait that appears consistently in all the great leaders of the Bible is that they were great in prayer. They were closely connected with You. As a result, You were more freely able to work through them to accomplish great things.

In Ephesians 3:20, I read that You are "able to do exceedingly abundantly above all that we ask or think, according to the power that works in us." A verse earlier, I see this is made possible in the person who is "filled with all the fullness of God." This describes a life of total surrender to You, a commitment I can make by yielding myself to You in prayer.

I believe it is correct to say my leadership will only be as good as my prayer life. If so, I want to pray more fervently. I don't want a lack of prayer to hold me back. I give myself wholly to You so that You may work through me however You desire!

The effective, fervent prayer
of a righteous man avails much.

JAMES 5:16

My Time Belongs to Jesus

Jesus, I want to view my time as Your time. When I surrendered my life to You and asked You to become my Savior and Lord, I placed You on the throne of my life. Yet I admit there are times I don't act like You are my King—times when I usurp Your rightful authority for selfish reasons.

In light of the great love and mercy You have shown me, Romans 12:1 urges me to be a living sacrifice—to stay on the altar yielded to Your purposes and not jump down to do my own thing. May the ways I use my time reflect that I am a servant who is eager to fulfill Your calling for me. Help me to have a mindset and attitudes that seek to do Your will with great gladness.

Enable me to look at my schedule through Your eyes so that I can make my time count more toward the things of eternity.

The world is passing away, and the lust of it;
but he who does the will of God abides forever.

1 JOHN 2:17

Prayer Wisdom

The whole point of living a praying life is to be close to God and to have a deep, solid, and unshakeable relationship with Him. A praying life allows you to be solidly aligned with the Lord by communing and communicating with Him throughout each day. This means not only knowing *about* God, but truly knowing *Him*—or at least as much as He can be known on this earth.

Knowing God starts with the *desire* to know Him and then *seeking* to know Him. From there it becomes a matter of wanting *more and more* of Him in your heart and in your life. The focus isn't on the praying. The focus is on the *One to whom you are praying.*[10]

STORMIE OMARTIAN

Working Wholeheartedly

Father, there are times when, as I carry out my leadership responsibilities, I find myself merely going through the motions. For some reason or other, I find myself distracted, complacent, or eager to move on. My heart isn't in what I'm doing.

When that happens, Lord, awaken me to the fact that my complacency dulls my performance. Remind me that others are watching the example I set. The last thing I want is for my half-hearted leadership to affect my coworkers negatively.

As I lead, may I remember that every part of my workday is a service to You, and therefore I want to give my best. You are a Lord of excellence, and I want my work to reflect that. When I view You as the ultimate judge of my efforts, I am inspired to do better. At the end of each day, I want to be able to lift up the results of my labors as an offering that pleases You.

This is a faithful saying, and these things I want you to affirm constantly, that those who have believed in God should be careful to maintain good works. These things are good and profitable to men.

TITUS 3:8

My Calling as a Leader

LEADING WITH GREAT FAITH

Lord, when it comes to measuring my growth as a leader, my first inclination is to look at increased performance and productivity. But I also want to evaluate whether my faith in You has increased too. For when I have greater faith, that has a positive ripple effect on all else that I do.

Thank You for giving me the Scriptures so that, in reading them, I can grow my faith. Every page proclaims that You are worthy of all my trust. As I see the ways in which Abraham, Ruth, David, Mary, and many others grew in their faith because of Your works in their lives, my faith grows too. And as I read, meditate upon, and witness the fulfillment of Your many promises to me, my faith deepens all the more.

Help me to go beyond merely leading well. I want to lead well with great faith. May I guard my times alone with You and Your Word so my faith can increase.

The just shall live by faith.

HEBREWS 10:38

NO LEADER IS INDISPENSABLE

Lord, if there is one mistake that's easy for me to make, it's to assume I'm indispensable for the role I fill. If I like the thought there is no one who can fill my shoes, then maybe I need to change the way I do leadership.

It's not healthy for me to think I'm irreplaceable. No one lives forever. Times change. And different skill sets are needed to keep an organization thriving.

If a crisis were to occur upon my departure, then I haven't done my job of training and equipping people who can help ensure a smooth transition. Give me a vision for doing what is necessary for the good of this workplace, and not myself. The almighty Moses didn't lead Israel into the Promised Land—You gave that task to Joshua, whom You had prepared. As I lead, help me to find the Joshuas I can trust and develop with the confidence that change is inevitable—and beneficial.

After the death of Moses the servant of the LORD,
it came to pass that the LORD spoke to Joshua...saying:
"Moses My servant is dead. Now therefore, arise,
go over this Jordan, you and all this people,
to the land which I am giving to them."

JOSHUA 1:1-2

PART 3

MY CHARACTER
AS A LEADER

SELFLESS

Lord, the most selfless leader who ever lived was You. In all that You did, You demonstrated what it means to lead by giving Yourself up completely for others. As Philippians 2 says, You made Yourself of no reputation, took on the form of a bondservant, and humbled Yourself in obedience—to the point of death! (verses 7-8). You did all that for the good of Your followers.

As I evaluate my leadership, may I not be afraid to ask: Am I watching out for myself, or for those whom I lead? Am I preoccupied with my own needs, or am I alert to the needs of others? Am I eager for people to praise me, or am I glad to point the spotlight on them?

When You left Your throne in heaven to serve on this earth and die on the cross, You paid the ultimate sacrifice for our good. As I lead others, may I be willing to sacrifice myself so they may benefit.

The Son of Man did not come to be served, but to serve, and to give His life a ransom for many.

MARK 10:45

FAITHFUL IN THE LITTLE THINGS

Lord, I admit sometimes I feel as though I'm not getting the breaks I need to move on to bigger opportunities as a leader. I've had goals I want to achieve, but for some reason or another, they seem as distant as ever.

When I find myself in that place, help me to remember what You taught in Luke 16:10: "If you are faithful in little things, you will be faithful in large ones" (NLT). Proving my ability to handle lesser responsibilities prepares me for the greater ones. Rather than lament my unfulfilled dreams about the future, may I find joy and contentment in learning ways to get better at what I'm doing now.

I don't want to run ahead of Your plans for my life, Lord. May I gladly do today's work well so I am building bridges that will keep me moving forward. As I do this, I will grow in patience, perseverance, and faith.

> I waited patiently for the LORD;
> And He inclined to me,
> And heard my cry.
>
> **PSALM 40:1**

SPEAKING THE TRUTH IN LOVE

Father, there are times when it is painful to speak the truth, and it's tempting to tell a partial lie to protect myself or to avoid hurting others. It's easy to get caught up in figuring out how to find a "middle ground" where I don't have to tell the complete truth, but I can also avoid telling a complete lie.

Help me to recognize when I'm rationalizing my words because I am afraid to be entirely truthful. As a leader, I realize the people around me need to have the assurance my words can be trusted. For if they have reason to doubt my speech, they also have reason to doubt my actions—and my leadership.

Before I talk with others, examine my heart, Lord, and instruct me so that I will speak "the truth in love" (Ephesians 4:15). And I know that as I do so, I will have a clear conscience before You...and those around me.

He who speaks truth declares righteousness.

PROVERBS 12:17

A True Leader Serves

Lord, in the course of Your ministry, You made it clear that true leadership is all about giving of ourselves to others. You demonstrated that we are to pour ourselves into the lives of those around us—and that doing so can come with a cost. Though You are the King of kings and therefore You are the ultimate leader and authority over every creature on earth, You said that You came to serve, not to be served (Mark 10:45). May that be my ambition as well!

As I lead, may I do so with a willingness to sacrifice of myself for the benefit of others. And may I do so cheerfully! May I never complain about the cost and difficulty of being a leader. Rather, I want to be grateful for the privilege of being able to live out Your example to those around me.

> Whoever desires to become great among you shall be your servant.
>
> **MARK 10:43**

THE LEADER GOD USES

Lord, there are days when I am very aware of my flaws and shortcomings. At times I am filled with doubts about my ability to be the leader I ought to be.

But then I am reminded of 1 Samuel 13:14: "The LORD has sought out a man after his own heart and appointed him ruler of his people" (NIV). From this I learn that when a heart is fully yielded to You, You are able to make use of that person. May that be true about my heart—may I be fully surrendered to You so that You can work through me unhindered.

When I give myself over to You as a vessel of Your work, then I know Your strengths can compensate for my weaknesses. May I then make a habit of offering my heart, mind, labors, and goals to You. Make me a leader after Your heart—one who seeks to please You in all that I do so You are free to work through me however You want.

Acquaint yourself with Him, and be at peace;
Thereby good will come to you.
Receive, please, instruction from His mouth,
And lay up His words in your heart.

JOB 22:21-22

AUTHORITY AND HUMILITY

Lord, in all that You did as the ultimate example of a leader, You struck the perfect balance between authority and humility. You showed strength and resolve as well as a heart of service and love.

In the attempt to be liked by those around me, it's easy to relax the standards, to accept less than what is ideal. Yet I realize that when my leadership is weak, people won't be challenged to give their best. Help me to figure out how to exercise my authority in ways that will spur excellence, and yet balance that with a compassion that lets others know I truly care about them. I realize people will flourish only to the extent I provide decisive, strong leadership. May I not be afraid to be that kind of leader.

Refresh within me an awareness that rightly expressed authority gives people clarity, direction, and a reason to aim high. And when it's tempered with love, then it's a positive and godly kind of authority.

If I...your Lord and Teacher, have washed your feet,
you also ought to wash one another's feet.
For I have given you an example,
that you should do as I have done to you.

JOHN 13:14-15

PRAYER WISDOM

Prayer is the only entryway into genuine self-knowledge. It is also the main way we experience deep change—the reordering of our loves. Prayer is how God gives us so many of the unimaginable things he has for us. Indeed, prayer makes it safe for God to give us many of the things we most desire. It is the way we know God, the way we finally treat God as God.[11]

TIMOTHY KELLER

A SERVANT LEADER

Father, in today's world, the word "servant" doesn't spur much respect. Culture places little value on those who work in servant roles, viewing them as occupants at the bottom of society's pecking order.

But You esteem servants to be the greatest of all! You declared, "Whoever desires to become great among you shall be your servant" (Mark 10:43). That is so contrary to what the world teaches!

As I lead, Lord, may I listen not to what the world says, but what You say. May I remember Your example in the upper room, where You washed Your disciples' feet shortly before You went to the cross. Though You are the Lord of the universe, You lovingly performed a task that belongs to the lowest of the low.

As a leader, then, may I bear the label "servant" with joy!

He who is greatest among you shall be your servant.

MATTHEW 23:11

Exercising Authority with Grace

Father, when it comes to leading those around me, help me to have patience. Remind me that growth, change, and the gaining of experience are all day-by-day processes that take time. May I be the kind of boss who knows how to set objectives and goals that are both reasonable and challenging. And may I possess the kind of sensitivity that discerns when matters outside the workplace might affect someone's performance.

When it comes to patience, I think about the tremendous grace You've shown to me. Sometimes You've tried to teach me a lesson and I haven't been attentive. Or I've allowed my preoccupation with work to crowd You out, and I'm moving forward in my own strength and wisdom instead of seeking Yours.

In the same way that Your patience abounds with me, may my patience abound with others. May I clearly exhibit grace even as I exercise authority and uphold expectations.

Blessed are the merciful, for they shall obtain mercy.

MATTHEW 5:7

LEADING WITH HUMILITY

Lord, when I prosper in my work, I know that it is because You have equipped me and blessed me. You have made me what I am, and You get the glory for what I have accomplished. When compliments and praises are directed my way, may I lift them up to You.

Protect me from the all-too-human tendency to feed and satisfy my ego. In my role as a leader, I realize I'm vulnerable to puffed-up thoughts about myself or my importance. Just because I'm higher on the organizational chart doesn't mean I have higher value. I want to treat my coworkers as true equals—though we have different responsibilities, we are all needed to get the work done.

Should pride gain a foothold in me, call my attention to it. It's only when I remove pride that humility can reside in me. Remind me of Jesus's example of humble leadership, that I may walk as He did.

Search me, O God, and know my heart;
Try me, and know my anxieties;
And see if there is any wicked way in me,
And lead me in the way everlasting.

PSALM 139:23-24

NECESSITY OF A RIGHT PERSONAL LIFE

Father, how am I doing when it comes to caring for my responsibilities outside the workplace? If I were to do an honest assessment of how well I manage my marriage, family, home, spiritual life, and everything else that's personal, could I truly say all is well? If I were to ask You to reveal where I've been negligent or inadequate, what would You say?

As painful as the answers might be, please point them out. I want to be a good steward over *everything* You've entrusted to me. Open my eyes and heart to the specific changes I need to make.

I realize that if I'm not caring for my personal life, the effects can spill over into my work life. Convict me of the urgency of a well-maintained personal life so that You are pleased and my leadership has integrity.

The integrity of the upright will guide them,
But the perversity of the unfaithful will destroy them.

PROVERBS 11:3

Praying with Awareness

Jesus, as I pray for those who work with me, I want to do more than just utter their names and move on. Give me the kind of heart that desires to pray with awareness. Help me to pay attention, to listen, to cultivate a sensitivity that notices their areas of need or concern. May I also know about their jobs well enough that I can pray with wisdom for their responsibilities and how they can be supported.

In this way, Lord, I can show Your love. I can also grow to understand these persons better. They don't necessarily need to know that I am praying for them; I simply want to uphold them and learn how to care about them in the ways You do.

As I pray with awareness, may I also have a heart ready for ministry. If I sense You are opening a door for me to bring blessing into someone's life, may I walk through it willingly.

Continue earnestly in prayer,
being vigilant in it with thanksgiving.

COLOSSIANS 4:2

Imitating God's Patience

Father, in the same way that You have been patient with me, may I be patient with those around me. I marvel at Your gracious longsuffering toward me, which I know I don't deserve. There have been so many times that I've doubted You and expressed impatience because I fail to realize You really do care and know what is best for me. You have been steadfast in showing Your faithfulness during all the times I have been shortsighted.

When I feel impatient toward someone else, convict me with a reminder of Your patience toward me. When I wonder how I can possibly be patient, may I remember that Your patience with me was so great that even while I was your enemy, Your Son died for me (Romans 5:8). May I see any challenges to my patience as opportunities to imitate You and to bring calm, grace, and love into difficult situations.

As the elect of God, holy and beloved,
put on tender mercies, kindness,
humility, meekness, longsuffering.

COLOSSIANS 3:12

Leading with a Clear Conscience

Father, I realize that as a leader I am accountable not only to those who follow me, but also to You. While those who work with me day in and day out won't necessarily know the motives behind what I do or the condition of my heart, You do. As King David said in Psalm 139, "You have searched me and known me…and are acquainted with all my ways. For there is not a word on my tongue, but behold, O Lord, You know it altogether" (verses 1,3-4).

When it comes to carrying out my duties, I want to have a clear conscious before You. I want to lead with an ongoing awareness that nothing is hidden from You. Having that mindset will motivate me to examine my thoughts, decisions, words, and actions before I carry them out.

While the knowledge that I answer to You can be intimidating, I realize this kind of accountability will inspire better leadership. That makes it all worthwhile!

I know also, my God, that You test the heart and have pleasure in uprightness.

1 CHRONICLES 29:17

Prayer Wisdom

Stay with God in the secret place longer than we are with men in the public place and the fountain of our wisdom will never dry up. Keep our hearts open to the inflowing Spirit and we will not become exhausted by the outflow. Cultivate the acquaintance of God more than the friendship of men and we will always have abundance of bread to give to the hungry. Our first responsibility is not to the public but to God and our own souls.[12]

A.W. TOZER

A CONSISTENT SPIRITUAL LIFE

Lord, when it comes to my work life and home life, it's easy to compartmentalize the two. What I do for a living is one thing; what I do at my job is another. Much of what I do in the workplace isn't done at home, and vice versa.

But if there's one area where I need to be constant in both places, it's my spiritual life. When it comes to fulfilling my obligations, I need to be equally diligent in both worlds. It's not right for me to have a higher standard in one place than the other. My integrity, faithfulness, and convictions shouldn't diminish as I change from one setting to another.

If I am slipping in one realm or the other, please alert me. When it comes time for me to give You an account of all that You entrusted to me in both worlds, I want to be able to say I always gave my best.

Do not be deceived, God is not mocked;
for whatever a man sows, that he will also reap.
For he who sows to his flesh will of the flesh reap corruption,
but he who sows to the Spirit will of the Spirit
reap everlasting life.

GALATIANS 6:7-8

A Leader Who Can Be Trusted

Lord, I am grateful You are a God who keeps His every word. As 1 Kings 8:56 says, not one of Your good promises has failed. Whatever You say can be trusted. Because You are faithful, I have no need to worry that You won't follow through for me.

I want the same to be true about my words as a leader. I realize how important it is for my coworkers to know that whatever I say, I will do. For if I don't keep my word, that will open the door of doubt—bringing into question the integrity of anything else I say. And that, in turn, will undermine my ability to earn their confidence and lead effectively.

Before I make a commitment, help me to use discernment. Do I know for certain I can make it happen? And when I make a promise, convict me of the need to make sure I fulfill it. I want people to know they can count on me.

Let your "Yes" be "Yes," and your "No," "No,"
lest you fall into judgment.

JAMES 5:12

STAYING SPIRITUALLY HEALTHY

Father, give me the discernment I need to make sure I don't allow any problems in my work life to pull me down in my spiritual life. With the commitment I have to my job, it would be easy for the struggles I face there to have a demoralizing effect on me as a believer.

I am mindful of Your promise in 2 Peter 1:3 that You have given me "*all* things that pertain to life and godliness." In every way, You are my provider and sustainer so that I lack nothing. You are "my rock and my fortress and my deliverer" (Psalm 18:2), protecting me no matter what life throws at me.

When I take good care of my spiritual health, I am more likely to have a positive outlook no matter how negative things get at work. The better I stay connected to You, the better I will weather the storms in the workplace. The stronger I am spiritually, the stronger I'll be as a leader.

Be strong in the Lord and in the power of His might.

EPHESIANS 6:10

Representing God Well

Lord, as I do my job, may I always be conscious of the fact I am a representative of You. And because I'm in a position of leadership, those around me are likely to pay even closer attention to my words and actions than I realize.

In Your Scriptures You say, "Let your conduct be worthy of the gospel of Christ" (Philippians 1:27). A little later You add, "Do everything without complaining and arguing, so that no one can criticize you. Live clean, innocent lives as children of God, shining like bright lights in a world full of crooked and perverse people" (2:14-15 NLT).

As I go about my job each day, please bring these exhortations to mind. May I think before I act so I don't inadvertently behave in ways that will reflect negatively on You. I want my life to provide my coworkers with an accurate portrayal of You.

Walk worthy of the calling with which you were called.

EPHESIANS 4:1

Leading with Fairness

Father, I've learned from experience how easy it is for positive or negative relationships with certain people in the workplace to cloud a leader's ability to make the best decisions. I recognize the necessity of making sure my friendships with specific individuals don't impair my ability to guide the entire team with fairness. And I need to guard myself from allowing frustration or jealousy to unfairly affect the way I treat those who are doing their jobs well.

As I consider my decisions and actions, may I do so with wisdom and not my emotions. Enable me to see each situation clearly and prayerfully ask for Your guidance so that I don't play favorites or do harm. Alert me in those times when I find myself more concerned about pleasing people than doing what's right. Help me to treat the entire team with fairness and integrity so that I can lead well.

There is no partiality with God.

ROMANS 2:11

TREATING OTHERS KINDLY

Lord, there are some days when I just don't seem to get along with anyone. For whatever reason, even those who engage me in a positive manner get a grumpy response. I let my foul mood get in the way and I end up hurting people even though deep down, I know what I'm doing is wrong.

It's in times like these I need to be reminded not to allow my negative emotions or circumstances dictate how I treat others. Convict me of the importance of bringing my personal issues to You and placing them in Your hands rather than throwing them in other people's faces. You affirm it is possible for me to "rejoice in the Lord always" no matter what my situation (Philippians 4:4). My joy comes from my relationship with You, not what's happening around me. Help me to live in that joy even in the tough times so I can show kindness to everyone throughout the day.

As we have opportunity, let us do good to all.

GALATIANS 6:10

LEADING IN GOD'S POWER

Lord, some experts say leadership is about self-confidence. Authority. A get-it-done-at-any-cost mentality. A commanding presence. The ability to persuade. But as I ponder those characteristics, they have two things in common: the exaltation of self and control over others.

Nowhere in the Scriptures do I see those traits as part of Your definition of leadership. You seek out those who get their confidence and authority from You. Your Word calls for humility and dependence upon You. It commends putting others before self. It extols bearing the fruit of the Spirit rather than mere charm and persona.

Those are the differences between self-centered leadership and God-centered leadership. I know what kind of leader I want to be—one who walks in Your power rather than my own. May everything that I do as a leader make it clear to others that You are the source of my all.

You know that the rulers in this world lord it over their people, and officials flaunt their authority over those under them. But among you it will be different. Whoever wants to be a leader among you must be your servant, and whoever wants to be first among you must become your slave.

MATTHEW 20:25-27 NLT

PRAYER WISDOM

Prayer is the application of want to Him who alone can relieve it, the voice of sin to Him who alone can pardon it. It is the urgency of poverty, the prostration of humility, the fervency of penitence, the confidence of trust. It is not eloquence, but earnestness; not figures of speech, but compunction of soul.[13]

HANNAH MORE

A LEADER WHO IS AVAILABLE

Lord, there are many staffers in the course of a workday who need my time and attention. Meetings, phone calls, emails, and spontaneous conversations—in every instance, it's necessary for me to shift gears, set aside what's in front of me, and mentally engage myself in a new way.

A lot of times I find it tough to make that transition. I might even respond with impatience because the interruption prevents me from dealing with other matters. Yet I feel terrible when that happens—after all, the people I'm hearing from are valued coworkers. Besides, there are plenty of times when the roles are reversed and I'm the intruder—and I know how much I appreciate my staff's willingness to be available when I call upon them.

Give me the strength and resolve to provide my full attention to those who need it. If I find myself feeling resentful at first, stir within me a determination to be patient and kind—to be the servant leader You have called me to be.

Do not forget to do good and to share,
for with such sacrifices God is well pleased.

HEBREWS 13:16

My Character as a Leader

THE SPIRIT-LED LEADER

Lord, as I lead others, I want to walk in the Spirit and not the flesh. I yield myself to Your Holy Spirit, who enables me to display the fruit of the Spirit: love, joy, peace, longsuffering, kindness, goodness, faithfulness, gentleness, and self-control (Galatians 5:22-23).

Teach me what it means to love others as You love them. How I can exhibit joy no matter what my circumstances. How I can experience peace in the middle of chaos and busyness. How I can show patience when I'm feeling the opposite. The difference that kindness and goodness can add when I exercise my authority. The benefit of faithfulness rather than impulsiveness. The value of gentleness when hard things need to be said. And the wisdom of self-control when temptations or challenges arise.

I marvel that it's Your Spirit who produces all this. As I set self aside, He bears the fruit. You call the Spirit my Helper, and He is a Helper indeed.

He who abides in Me, and I in him, bears much fruit.

JOHN 15:5

FAITHFULNESS VERSUS SUCCESS

Father, I want to experience success as a leader, but not for the wrong reasons. Your definition of success is radically different from the world's, which I hear and read about constantly. Help me to silence the clamor of so-called human wisdom and listen instead to Your small voice of perfect and divine wisdom. I want to shape my leadership according to what You have to say.

This makes me recognize the importance of setting aside time to carefully evaluate what I'm doing and why. Prompt me, Lord, to check my motives, examine my goals, and reset myself so that my desires are shaped by Yours. Help me to be honest with myself so that I can purge from within the things that do not line up with Your will. I want to have motives and goals that are right and pure. It is faithfulness I want to be known for, not success.

It is required in stewards that one be found faithful.

1 CORINTHIANS 4:2

PLEASING GOD

Lord, as I lead and work together with others to get things done, I've noticed that sometimes my motive for doing so is to gain people's approval. I'm seeking fulfillment from the praise of others, which, if I'm not careful, can lead me into the mindset of thinking my value is based on how well I perform for them.

But human approval can be fickle. I might find myself in favor one day, and out of favor the next. By contrast, Your love for me is not based on how I perform, but on the fact You really do love me. Yours is an unconditional love that never wavers, even when I fail. That's why You alone are able to give me a true and lasting sense of value.

Thank You that even in the midst of my shortcomings, You are faithful. I don't have to worry that, on the days when I don't measure up, You'll abandon me. In all that I do in the workplace, then, may I seek fulfillment from doing what pleases You.

O LORD, You are my God.
I will exalt You,
I will praise Your name,
For You have done wonderful things.

ISAIAH 25:1

SPEAKING WITH GRACE

Father, Your Scriptures have much to say about good communication. You say that "the tongue has the power of life and death" (Proverbs 18:21 NIV). I am convicted as I realize my words can do great harm as well as great good. And their impact is magnified all the more by the fact I serve in a position of leadership.

May I take to heart the cry of the psalmist, who said, "Set a guard, O LORD, over my mouth; keep watch over the door of my lips" (Psalm 141:3). King Solomon—whom You gifted with great wisdom—observed, "A word fitly spoken is like apples of gold in settings of silver" (Proverbs 25:11).

When I speak, remind me of the need to choose my words carefully. Even in the times when I need to rebuke or admonish, may I do so in ways that build up rather than destroy. In every way, may my words bring grace to those who hear them (Ephesians 4:29).

Let your speech always be with grace.

COLOSSIANS 4:6

REPUTATION MATTERS

Father, Your Word says "a good name is to be chosen rather than great riches" (Proverbs 22:1). You call me to live blamelessly, without fault, as a light that shines to the world (Philippians 2:15). That is my heart's desire, for I want to bring honor to You and not reproach.

As I lead, help me to possess an ever-present awareness of the need to guard my reputation. In today's hyper-politically charged and post-Christian world, I realize my words and actions can easily be misunderstood or maligned. While I have no control over the possibility someone may bring unmerited accusations against me, I want to make a clearly visible effort to live uprightly with integrity at all times.

Make my heart sensitive to Your Spirit's leading all through the day. If I sense a call to caution, may I heed the Spirit's beckoning, no matter what the cost. I want to please You and protect how people view You.

> Let integrity and uprightness preserve me,
> For I wait for You.

PSALM 25:21

Mutual Self-Sacrifice

Father, as I read about the exploits of King David in Your Word, I marvel at the affection his mighty warriors had for him. Their loyalty was so great they were willing to die for him—because they knew David was willing to die for them. Between David and his men was a mutual willingness to true self-sacrifice.

While I realize my workplace is a totally different context—that I'm not in life-and-death military struggles as David was—I can see a valuable principle for leadership here: When I'm loyal to my followers, they're more likely to respond likewise. And I can imagine this kind of two-way commitment creates bonds that bring greater strength to all of us.

In the right times and situations, help me to thoughtfully search for ways I can demonstrate loyalty to my coworkers so that together, we can draw the best out of one another.

Be kind to one another, tenderhearted,
forgiving one another.

EPHESIANS 4:32

PRANER WISDOM

A spiritual prayer is that which leaves a spiritual mood behind upon the heart. A Christian is better after prayer. He has gained more strength over sin, as a man by exercise gets strength. The heart after prayer keeps a tincture of holiness…Having been with God on the mount—Moses' face shone. So, having been on the mount of prayer—our *graces* shine and our *lives* shine.[14]

THOMAS WATSON

BEING A GOOD LISTENER

Lord, in Your Scriptures, You advise, "Be quick to listen, slow to speak" (James 1:19 NIV). You place a premium on taking the time to hear and understand others. I can see how this might be hard for those in leadership positions because leaders tend to speak more than listen.

Yet I can see how being a good listener will help me be a better leader. When I am willing to listen, I am showing that I care. In this way I can earn trust, goodwill, and friendship. And there's another way of looking at this: If I don't listen, I won't have all the information I need to make the best decisions. I won't connect with people on their wavelength. A lack of interest on my part will undermine any spirit of cooperation I am hoping for from others.

Lord, the fact that You promise to hear all my prayers shows You are a dedicated listener who truly cares about me. May I follow Your example!

He who has knowledge spares his words,
And a man of understanding is of a calm spirit.

PROVERBS 17:27

STAYING HUMBLE

Father, I give You permission to humble me when I allow my stature as a leader to inflate my view of myself. Just because I wear a certain job title doesn't make me better than others. Nor does it increase my value in Your eyes.

I ask You to alert me when pride, arrogance, or any sense of self-importance gains a foothold within me. While I might enjoy a momentary flicker of satisfaction when I pat myself on the back, I realize that very quickly, such self-centeredness is certain to impair my ability to relate well to others—and to You.

As I kneel before You in prayer, may I fully repent of any prideful thoughts I have harbored recently. When others praise me, may I immediately turn that applause into thanks to You, and give You all the credit for making me what I am.

> I say, through the grace given to me,
> to everyone who is among you,
> not to think of himself more highly
> than he ought to think.
>
> **ROMANS 12:3**

Leading with Accountability

Lord, help me to lead with the knowledge that those who work for me are paying close attention to what I say and do. I might not want that to be the case, but it's a reality that comes with the fact they look to me for direction, help, and affirmation.

This makes accountability a two-way street. While my staff are responsible for doing their jobs well, I am responsible for the example I set. The way I lead can make a world of difference, affecting people positively or negatively.

Instill within me an awareness of how people respond to my leadership. While I can't always please everyone, I still want to lead to the best of my ability. Help me to reflect Your leadership style in my life. I know that when I make You my role model, I'll be the kind of example others can imitate.

To whom much is given, from him much will be required;
and to whom much has been committed,
of him they will ask the more.

LUKE 12:48

PART 4

My Challenges
as a Leader

Making the Best Decision

Heavenly Father, I am torn. I have a difficult decision to make, and I am struggling over which way to go. It's hard to know what I should do. Both options have their positives, but they also have their negatives. There are no easy answers.

My dilemma is made all the more challenging because people will be affected by this decision. I know not everyone will agree with me. I expect there will be some pushback, and that feelings will be hurt.

Help me to not only make the better choice, but to know the best way to move forward with sensitivity and resolve once the decision has been made. You have promised that when I am in need of wisdom, You will gladly give it. Fill me with Your wisdom now.

Trust in the LORD with all your heart,
And lean not on your own understanding;
In all your ways acknowledge Him,
And He shall direct your paths.

PROVERBS 3:5-6

WHEN I NEED PATIENCE
ABOUT THE FUTURE

Lord, my plans are not unfolding as I had anticipated. Things are not happening the way I had hoped. I admit I'm getting discouraged as the path forward becomes more uncertain.

As I struggle with doubt, help me to have patience. In my weariness, may I look to You for wisdom. As I wonder about what step I should take next, let me rest in You. The future is in Your hands, and I need to place myself in Your hands as well. There is no better place to be!

Though I cannot see what is to come, You know exactly what will happen next. Remind me to follow Your lead and not run ahead on my own. Calm my heart with the truth that You are Lord over all my tomorrows. May I be diligent to put You first, and trust that all else will fall into place as I do so.

> I sought the LORD, and He heard me,
> And delivered me from all my fears.

PSALM 34:4

IN GOD'S EYES, NO LITTLE THINGS

Father, as I fulfill my leadership role, I admit sometimes I'll rank certain tasks and people as being important or unimportant, worthy or insignificant, fitting for my stature or beneath me.

Yet You call me to be faithful in the little things so I can be trusted with the big things. Because everything I do is ultimately done for You, it all deserves my fullest attention, my best effort. In Your eyes, there is no person or responsibility that deserves less. From Your perspective, there are no little things.

Teach me to treasure my minutes as much as my hours, my entry-level workers as much as my top-level staff, my routine obligations as much as my career enhancers. Fill my heart with gratitude for everyone and everything so I never take them for granted. Whatever You have entrusted to me, I want to care for as You would.

Look at the birds of the air,
for they neither sow nor reap nor gather into barns;
yet your heavenly Father feeds them.

MATTHEW 6:26

BALANCING MY TIME

Father, I have so much to do. And on top of that, I have ideas and dreams about what I would like to accomplish. I have routine responsibilities that I realize must get done, and then there are the things I would rather be doing—projects I am truly excited about.

Help me to find the right balance, Lord. I know that if I don't take care of the day-to-day obligations, things will slip. And yet I don't want to lose sight of my hopes for the future, for they give me the motivation to keep moving forward, to keep growing.

Give me the discipline to plan ahead, create to-do lists, and get things done. Instill within me a desire to be a good steward of my hours. As I begin each day, give me the wisdom to determine my priorities, then carry them out—so that when evening comes, I know the satisfaction that comes from having used my time well.

Commit your works to the LORD,
and your plans will be established.

PROVERBS 16:3 ESV

WHEN DISCOURAGEMENT COMES

Father, I admit there are times when I feel like quitting. A major decision doesn't go the direction I had hoped. A disagreement with a coworker has left painful wounds. I made a poor decision that had negative consequences. I feel overlooked or underappreciated. Then there are those days when I just can't seem to do anything right.

When I'm feeling down, remind me to look up and turn my frustrations over to You. Help me to rise above my disappointment and circumstances, and to keep a check on my emotions so they don't pull me downward. In the difficult moments, remind me of what I need most: Your wisdom, Your grace, Your peace, Your comfort. No matter what my situation, You can provide exactly what I need.

Lord, when the hurt comes, may I reach out for Your healing. And may I refresh myself by focusing on—and pursuing—the goals, dreams, and hopes You have given me.

Be strong and do not let your hands be weak,
for your work shall be rewarded!

2 CHRONICLES 15:7

Prayer Wisdom

Only a good and wise and sovereign God would make prayer a duty and a privilege at the same time…Prayer is a privilege. It is not a burdensome duty. It is a wonderful privilege. Even though Scripture commands us to pray, we should not view prayer as something we *have* to do. We should view it as something we *get* to do.

It is a privilege to have an audience before the Creator and Sustainer of the universe. The blood and righteousness of the Lord Jesus Christ has given us access to the throne of grace. Every redeemed follower of Christ is granted an open door before the Lord Almighty.[15]

H.B. CHARLES JR.

LIVING PEACEABLY WITH OTHERS

Father, because every one of us humans are fallen creatures, I realize my interactions with others won't be free of problems. Conflict and disagreement are sure to occur. Frustration and disappointment are to be expected. All because our default mode—as humans—is our selfish and fleshly nature. And rather than assume that it's always others who are at fault, let me be quick to realize I have my own blind spots and am just as likely to be imperfect as anyone else.

So it makes sense that in Scripture, You urge me to live peaceably with others, to seek their best instead of my own, to be quick to listen and slow to speak, and to be willing to forgive. You even tell me to love my enemies (Matthew 5:44), which isn't easy! But that's exactly what You did as You hung on the cross. And because Your power resides within me, I know I can do all You have asked me to do when it comes to relating the best I possibly can to others.

If it is possible, as much as depends on you,
live peaceably with all men.

ROMANS 12:18

TRUSTING THE GOD WHO
SEES AND RULES ALL

Lord, from Your heavenly throne, You are able to see all things with perfect clarity. From Your high place, You can see not only what is happening now, but what will take place in the future. And as Psalm 121:4 says, You neither slumber nor sleep. You are ever alert.

Not only do You have a clear perspective, but You are sovereign over what the future holds. As Isaiah 46:11 says, You have determined Your purpose, and You will bring it to pass.

Knowing these truths brings me great comfort. Though I may be uncertain about what lies ahead, I have no reason to worry. You are already present in all my tomorrows. Everything is securely in Your hands. May I place myself in Your hands as well, and fully yield myself to Your leading. May I lean not on my own understanding, but trust in You to direct my paths.

> The LORD is in his holy temple;
> the LORD's throne is in heaven;
> his eyes see.
>
> **PSALM 11:4 ESV**

ALERT FOR GOD'S BLESSINGS

Lord, there are days when, as a leader, I feel like I am walking two steps forward, then three steps back. As I finish one task, two more pop up. As I earnestly meet one deadline, new ones arise unexpectedly. In the midst of how busy I get, it's easy for me to dwell on what's going wrong instead of what's going right.

In the day-to-day rush of getting my work done, remind me to pause and notice the blessings You have sent my way. When a meeting goes well, a task gets done right, a coworker speaks a word of encouragement, a budget is met, a solution is found, an idea bears fruit, a work relationship is strengthened—whatever it may be, may I recognize it and express thankfulness to You. For when I face even my most difficult days with a grateful spirit, I am enabled to keep my focus upward on You rather than on my problems.

Bless the LORD, O my soul,
And forget not all His benefits.

PSALM 103:2

WHEN FACING OPPOSITION

Father, I have a responsibility I've been putting off because I'm not looking forward to doing it. I've procrastinated, finding every excuse to delay action because I know this task will be unpleasant or painful.

Yet I realize that part of being a leader is being able to keep moving forward even in the face of a tough crisis or strong opposition. I need to accept the fact there will be times when I must deal with fallout or take a lonely stand for doing what is right or best.

When I am in that place, may I take solace in You. May I ask You first for wisdom, which You promise to supply. May I line myself up with Your Word, which is my sure foundation when all else is sinking sand. May I speak and act with grace and integrity so that even those who disagree with me will recognize that above all, I want to do what is right and honorable.

We are hard-pressed on every side, yet not crushed;
we are perplexed, but not in despair;
persecuted, but not forsaken;
struck down, but not destroyed.

2 CORINTHIANS 4:8-9

Finding Contentment

Lord, there are times when I find myself wishing I had a skill or talent someone else has. Or when I am envious about another person's successes and achievements. Help me to realize that when I compare myself to others, I've placed myself in a battle I am guaranteed to lose. You've gifted me to be different from others for a reason: so that I can carry out *Your* unique purpose for me. You have specific plans for how You want to use me, and You've equipped me accordingly.

Rather than pursue a path meant for someone else, may I take joy in where You lead me. Instead of measuring myself against others, may I measure myself against what You've asked of me. For when I do, I'll experience contentment. I'll know the peace that comes from abiding in Your perfect design for me—a design no one else can fulfill.

Not that I speak in regard to need,
for I have learned in whatever state I am, to be content.

PHILIPPIANS 4:11

ONE DAY AT A TIME

Lord, I am truly pressed for time these days. There is so much that demands my attention. I'm struggling to keep up with it all. And I've been cutting corners where I don't want to—such as my time spent with You or sacrificing on the quality of my work.

The constant grind has made me weary, and I'm tired of being tired. It's at times like this I realize I have my limitations and I need to figure out solutions. Give me clarity of mind as I look at my schedule. And enable me to ask the tough questions: What are my true priorities? Are my expectations unrealistic? Do I need to delegate more? What can I let go of? Would it help to get counsel from others?

Calm my heart, Lord. Help me to take one day at a time, to put You first, and to finish each day with the fulfillment that comes from knowing I have done what You called me to do.

Don't worry about tomorrow,
for tomorrow will bring its own worries.
Today's trouble is enough for today.

MATTHEW 6:34 NLT

Prayer Wisdom

Yes, I pray that my pain might be removed, that it might cease; but more so, I pray for the strength to bear it, the grace to benefit from it, and the devotion to offer it up to God as a sacrifice of praise.[16]

JONI EARECKSON TADA

DOING MY WORK WELL

Father, I realize that when I'm eager to bring forth results on a project—especially one that is new and exciting to me—there is always a danger that I could rush too quickly and shortchange myself, others, and the task at hand.

In such times, help me to view patience as a friend—one who will encourage me to discipline myself and take the time to do the job well. May I challenge myself to search out the best possible path forward for achieving the desired results. Help me to look at my work from all angles so that I can be certain the project is given every opportunity for success.

Very simply, I don't want to mess up because I was in a hurry. As I consider the works of Your hands, I see that You are a masterful Creator who takes joy in doing everything well—down to the smallest detail. May I be inspired by Your example.

Serve wholeheartedly,
as if you were serving the Lord, not people.

EPHESIANS 6:7 NIV

RESPONDING TO CRITICISM

Lord, when I am at the receiving end of criticism, give me the discernment to know how to respond. Were the words spoken harshly as if in ignorance or anger? Or is it possible the person has a valid point and I just don't want to hear it? Or maybe it's a mixture of both—the words were spoken recklessly, yet there's a concern I really do need to act upon.

As I consider what was said, help me not to overreact or speak thoughtlessly in return. Nor should I let another's opinion undermine me; You are my security and You know my heart. Enable me to separate the emotions of the moment from the facts at hand. If the criticism is legitimate, I want to use it well. In every instance, may I respond to strong words with prayer, wisdom, and kindness.

The ear that hears the rebukes of life
Will abide among the wise.

PROVERBS 15:31

PRESERVING UNITY IN CONFLICT

Father, I agree there is wisdom in numbers, but sometimes I wonder about that because it's so hard to get people to agree with one another! I get frustrated when, during a meeting, the discussion spins out of control. Everyone feels strongly about their perspective, and we end up with a conflict that brings work to a standstill. Decisions can't be made, and cooperation is replaced by disruption.

When that happens, Lord, calm my heart and remind me that Your Word calls me to be a peacemaker. Help me not to contribute to the fray, but to exercise self-control and to speak thoughtfully with grace. In spite of the disagreement at hand, may I seek to have a conciliatory spirit toward everyone involved. And regardless of whether or not I agree with the outcome, may I determine to maintain good relations and fulfill my job role the best I can.

Whatever you want men to do to you, do also to them.

MATTHEW 7:12

Choosing Words with Care

Father, I realize the damage careless words can do. I've had my fair share of comments I wish I could take back. And I've been hurt by verbal barbs that have been directed at me.

Yet even with that awareness, I still find myself all too easily blurting out thoughts I should hold back. Words escape my lips that weren't surrendered to You first. You urge me to take every thought captive to You (2 Corinthians 10:5). You also say, "Do not let any unwholesome talk come out of your mouths, but only what is helpful for building others up according to their needs, that it may benefit those who listen" (Ephesians 4:29 NIV).

Teach me, Lord, to choose my words with care, knowing that the good or harm they do can last days, weeks, and even longer after they're spoken.

The heart of the righteous studies how to answer.

PROVERBS 15:28

STAYING CONNECTED

Father, with so much work demanding my attention, and given my determination to get things done, I realize I can become so preoccupied that I am oblivious to what is happening to those who work for me. I can become so wrapped up in my own world that I fail to notice the needs or concerns of others. And I realize that if I don't make the effort to be available or communicate regularly, little problems can quickly turn into big ones.

Instead of waiting and expecting others to approach me, prompt me to make a habit of checking with them and asking what I can do to help. Stir within me a genuine desire to watch out for my staff as much as I watch out for myself. For I know that when I take good care of those under my charge, I am also taking good care of the workplace as a whole.

All the law is fulfilled in one word, even in this:
"You shall love your neighbor as yourself."

GALATIANS 5:14

SEEKING SOLUTIONS INSTEAD OF SCAPEGOATS

Lord, when things go wrong, I know how quickly we as humans fall into the blame game—myself included. The first impulse is to search for the culprit elsewhere. Surely it was someone else's fault and not mine!

But in the same way that I'm glad to take part of the credit when success comes, I realize that, as a leader, I need to be willing to share in the blame when failure happens. Force me to be honest with myself when I need to own up to my mistakes. And rather than devote my energy to searching for scapegoats, may I use it instead to build up others and help them work together to set things right.

To the extent that I'm willing to share the blame, Lord, I realize I am encouraging solutions rather than fear. And I am exhibiting a heart of humility rather than pride.

He who earnestly seeks good finds favor.

PROVERBS 11:27

Blessed Are the Peacemakers

Father, I recognize that a must-have trait of every good leader is a willingness to listen to others. It's only when people have confidence that I welcome their input that they will know they are valued.

Yet asking people to speak up makes me vulnerable to opinions I might not like. I admit I'm not comfortable with handling opposition, but resolving it is yet another trait of every good leader. That means I need to be willing to receive pushback without taking offense.

Your Word says, "Blessed are the peacemakers" (Matthew 5:9)—those who are conciliatory and pursue unity. In the times when disagreement arises, help me to make every effort to be tactful and gracious. And grant me the wisdom to know how to resolve discord for the good of everyone involved.

Always be humble and gentle.
Be patient with each other,
making allowance for each other's faults
because of your love.

EPHESIANS 4:2 NLT

Prayer Wisdom

No issue or problem should ever be seen as too small for seeking God's input. The next time you are considering something "obvious," something that seems to be so clear-cut as to not require prayer, think again…and quickly get down on your knees and cry out to God.[17]

JIM GEORGE

Raising People Up

Lord, there are so many fine lines to walk as a leader! As I evaluate my leadership, give me the discernment to recognize whether I am merely *directing* people or truly *developing* them.

Am I simply telling them what to do, or am I giving them ownership of their jobs and the opportunity to grow? Am I merely making use of people, or do I genuinely value their contributions? Am I worried that others will outshine me, or am I thrilled when they reach levels of competency that exceed mine? Am I requiring them to be dependent upon me, or am I equipping them with the resources to be self-sufficient in their roles? When my workers fall short, am I critical of them, or do I bring encouragement?

In every way, Lord, I want to be the kind of leader who develops people, lifts them upward, and gives them every opportunity to know fulfillment from their work.

Let no one seek his own,
but each one the other's well-being.

1 CORINTHIANS 10:24

A DELIBERATE FOCUS ON TODAY

Father, as I look at my calendar, I find myself becoming distracted by the obligations that loom ahead of me. I see commitments and deadlines filling up the horizon, and if I am not careful, my efforts and energies for today can become drained by worries about tasks that are still future.

While there is wisdom in preparing for what is to come, at the same time, help me to concentrate on what needs my most immediate attention—the people and projects for today. I want to finish this day well so that tomorrow is a clean slate, another opportunity to be a good steward of what You have entrusted to me. While I am mindful of tomorrow, enable me to stay fully focused on today. Then at the end of the day I can present the results to You with the knowledge I gave my best. And my sense of accomplishment will give me the confidence I need to overcome the anxieties I have about projects I have yet to start.

May he give you the desire of your heart
and make all your plans succeed.

PSALM 20:4 NIV

WHEN I DON'T KNOW WHAT TO DO

Lord, I am feeling overwhelmed. I have a situation before me that is making me anxious. I don't see a clear solution yet, and I'm not even sure if I can figure out the best way forward.

At times like this, I need to remember there is no better place to put a problem than in Your hands. I give this fully to You, resting in the promise that when I make my requests known, You'll fill me with the peace that surpasses all understanding (Philippians 4:6-7). As I struggle to understand, the one thing I need most is Your peace.

Though I do not know the eventual outcome of this dilemma, You do. Help me to rest in the truths that You are sovereign and that You know what is best for Your children. May I place my full confidence in You rather than in myself.

Humble yourselves under the mighty hand of God,
that He may exalt you in due time,
casting all your care upon Him,
for He cares for you.

1 PETER 5:6-7

Past and Future Faithfulness

Father, when I find myself up against a seemingly impossible circumstance, refresh my memory of the times in the past when You have gotten me through other tough challenges. When the psalmist was overwhelmed by doubt over Your provision in his time of need, he wrote, "I will remember the works of the LORD; surely I will remember Your wonders of old. I will also meditate on all Your work, and talk of Your deeds" (Psalm 77:11-12).

Your faithfulness to me in the past is a sure confirmation You will remain faithful to me in the future. When I have no idea how I'm going to resolve a problem, remind me to take my eyes off myself and turn them to You. And rather than cling to my expectations for what the solution should be, may I trust You to do Your work in Your timing. As almighty God, You have the entire universe in Your sovereign care, and that means You have my life in Your care as well.

Fear the LORD, and serve Him in truth with all your heart;
for consider what great things He has done for you.

1 SAMUEL 12:24

Prayer as a First Resort

Father, I know the human tendency to first expend all sorts of effort on resolving a difficult problem before giving up and, as a last resort, coming to You in prayer. I too have been guilty of struggling without giving any thought of asking You for help.

In Hebrews 4:16, You have given me a standing invitation to come boldly before Your throne of grace to find help in time of need. First Peter 5:7 urges me to cast all my anxieties upon You, and Philippians 4:6 reminds me that "in everything by prayer and supplication, with thanksgiving, let your requests be made known to God." At all times, You are just a prayer away.

When trouble arises, may my first reaction be to come before You in prayer. I want to be a leader marked by God-sufficiency rather than self-sufficiency. Help me to make a habit of inviting Your involvement from the start!

Seek the LORD and His strength;
Seek His face evermore!

1 CHRONICLES 16:11

Defeat as a Learning Experience

Lord, when I lead, I realize things won't always go the way I hoped. There will be times when defeat comes. In fact, it's certain—which is why I need to learn how to handle disappointment well.

In the times when circumstances are completely beyond my control, help me to let go and not blame myself. But when it really is my fault—I made a poor choice, I didn't plan ahead, or I made outright mistakes—give me the integrity and courage to admit my error.

Yet no matter what happened and why, rather than let defeat get me down, may I look to it as a learning experience that will make me wiser. Give me the determination to pick myself up, get back on track, and exercise better leadership. Rather than let the fires of defeat destroy me, may I use them to refine me.

Fear not, for I am with you;
Be not dismayed, for I am your God.
I will strengthen you,
Yes, I will help you,
I will uphold you with My righteous right hand.

ISAIAH 41:10

WHEN IN NEED OF RENEWAL

Lord, I've been so busy that lately I've been slogging my way through the workday. The overload is affecting me, and it's been hard to generate enthusiasm or feel productive. I don't like feeling this way because I don't want to have a negative impact on those around me.

Will You please help refresh me? Renew my energy. Help me to set aside the things that don't really need my attention right now—and to let go of past concerns I've allowed to weigh me down. As I lighten my burdens and reconsider my true priorities, I'll become more focused.

Above all, may I take time to rest and let You restore my strength for the demands I face each day. It starts, of course, by spending time alone with You. Calm my heart and mind, and protect me from feeling overwhelmed. With You at my side, I know my every need will be met.

Blessed is the man who trusts in the LORD,
And whose hope is in the LORD.
For he shall be like a tree planted by the waters,
Which spreads out its roots by the river,
And will not fear when heat comes;
But its leaf will be green,
And will not be anxious in the year of drought,
Nor will cease from yielding fruit.

JEREMIAH 17:7-8

PRAYER WISDOM

God always acts positively when a believer lays a situation of need before him, but he does not always act in the way or at the speed asked for. In meeting the need, he does what he knows to be best when he knows it is best to do it…Christ's words to Paul, "My grace is sufficient for you, for my power is made perfect in weakness," when Paul had sought healing for his thorn in the flesh (2 Cor 12:7-9) meant no, but not simply no. Though it was not what Paul had expected, it was a promise of something better than the healing he had sought. We too may ask God to change situations and find that what he does instead is to give us strength to bear them unchanged. But this is not a simple no; it is a very positive answer to our prayer.[18]

J.I. PACKER

GIVING CREDIT WHERE IT IS DUE

Father, thank You for upholding me as I waited on the outcome of this long and difficult process. There were times when I got discouraged and even felt like giving up. I wondered if all my effort would go to waste. But I was truly surprised by the end result, which was favorable in more ways than I expected!

Thank You for helping me to endure and for allowing me the privilege of enjoying the taste of victory. As I struggled with uncertainty and doubt, You kept me moving forward. Because of the supernatural ways in which You enable me, I'm sure I don't recognize the extent to which You are working through me. But one thing I do know: You get the credit for sustaining me the entire way through this winding journey. All my praise goes to You!

Now to Him who is able to do exceedingly abundantly above all that we ask or think, according to the power that works in us, to Him be glory in the church by Christ Jesus to all generations, forever and ever.

EPHESIANS 3:20-21

SEASONS OF WAITING ON GOD

Father, I'm struggling with a lot of uncertainty right now. Some plans I've worked on are at a standstill. I'm anxious to keep moving forward but I can't because there's no clear solution. The irony of all this is that leaders are expected to fix problems, and I've got a problem I can't fix.

It's at times like this that I need to remember that seasons of waiting on You can have a good purpose. Most likely the reason an answer hasn't come is because the time or the circumstances aren't right. There are pieces of the puzzle that still need to fall into place. There are things I need to learn, in patience, that I otherwise wouldn't learn.

As I find it necessary to wait, teach me the value of patience. Calm my heart and rest my fears. Help me to see whether I'm really trusting You as I should. You've said You are watching over me and will guide me. I believe, Lord.

> The LORD is good to those who wait for Him,
> To the soul who seeks Him.
>
> **LAMENTATIONS 3:25**

THE BEST POLICY IN CONFLICT

Father, when conflict happens in the workplace, give me the discernment I need to resolve it the right way.

Sometimes a problem seems to have an obvious solution because I've only heard one side of the issue. Equip me with patience and restraint as I seek out all the facts before I make decisions or judgments. Give me the sensitivity to recognize that when people are involved, feelings are as well. As I work toward an answer, I have to accept the strong possibility that not everyone will be happy. That's when I need to remember: Speaking the truth in love (Ephesians 4:15) is always the best policy. Truth is always right, and love—even in the midst of disagreement—encourages cooperation instead of animosity.

When it comes to dealing with tensions at work, provide me with the balance and discernment necessary to bring about the best possible outcome.

Give thought to what is honorable in the sight of all.

ROMANS 12:17 ESV

Staying Calm When Chaos Hits

Lord, if there's one thing that really throws me out of my comfort zone as a leader, it's when circumstances fly out of control. It's hard for me to deal with uncertainty and not knowing how to restore order.

When that happens, I need to rest in the truth that You are always in control. Nothing ever takes You by surprise. Whereas I cannot see the light at the end of the tunnel, You already know the outcome. Just because my plans have gone haywire doesn't mean Yours have too. I can already see, then, a benefit to my feelings of inadequacy—they drive me to greater dependence upon You, which is exactly what You want.

Thank You, Lord, for the calm that fills my heart when I remember You are totally sovereign. You are Lord over all. You are God, and I am not. This replaces my anxiety with peace and my fear with confidence. I will trust You to sustain and preserve me.

> The LORD is my strength and my shield;
> My heart trusted in Him, and I am helped;
> Therefore my heart greatly rejoices,
> And with my song I will praise Him.
>
> **PSALM 28:7**

The Wisdom of Planning Ahead

Lord, finding enough time to get everything done is a constant challenge. While it's easy to view time as an adversary, I realize that's actually not the case. Time is a constant; everyone is given the same amount. As I think more carefully about this, I see it's really a matter of discipline. Every waking hour of every day is an opportunity for me to use time well or waste it.

When I find myself aimlessly wondering what I should do next, that's a sign I haven't planned ahead. Instill within me the habit of looking forward and decisively determining what needs to get done, and when. Then I won't let time slip through the cracks—time I cannot recover because once it's behind me, it's gone.

Help me to view time as a friend who encourages me to be a wise planner. Above all, thank You for each day You grant for me to live through. When I use time well, that becomes an expression of my gratitude to You.

Teach us to number our days,
That we may gain a heart of wisdom.

PSALM 90:12

WHEN I FEEL INADEQUATE

Father, there are times when I feel inadequate as a leader. Recently some things haven't turned out as well as I had hoped. And that has led me to question my abilities.

Yet I cannot deny that You've made it possible for me to be where I am. As I look to the past, I remember the many ways You've orchestrated circumstances for my benefit. You've opened doors I couldn't have opened. And the more I think about it, the more I realize You've uniquely gifted me for the job I have.

It's in the times when I get discouraged that I need to keep the big picture in mind and not get bogged down by recent failures or obstacles. Inspire me with the determination to keep moving forward through both the ups and downs I face. Above all, may I cultivate a constant thankfulness for where You have placed me, for I know it's where You want me.

Though he fall, he shall not be utterly cast down;
For the LORD upholds him with His hand.

PSALM 37:24

TWO CHOICES

Lord, I admit I get anxious when a decision is in someone else's hands and I have no say in the outcome. As a leader, I'm used to having a voice in what happens. But when I don't, I feel helpless or frustrated.

Anytime I'm in that spot, I realize I have two choices: I can worry, or I can trust You. Just because something is out of my control doesn't mean it's out of Yours. Perhaps I won't like the final decision, but I know You are wiser than me. You may have a purpose I don't see yet. Besides, in the same way I desire cooperation from others, I should be willing to return the favor.

Teach me to be willing to let go when I need to. Flexibility is a desirable trait—especially when it comes to doing Your will and not mine. Rather than let any outcome disappoint me, may I derive joy from keeping my eyes on You.

Those who know Your name will put their trust in You;
For You, LORD, have not forsaken those who seek You.

PSALM 9:10

PRAYER WISDOM

Sometimes we think we are too busy to pray. That is a great mistake, for praying is a saving of time…If we have no time we must make time, for if God has given us time for secondary duties, He must have given us time for the primary ones, and to draw near to Him is a primary duty, and we must let nothing set it on one side…Your other engagements will run smoothly if you do not forget your engagement with God.[19]

C.H. SPURGEON

Lonely at the Top

Lord, being a leader is often a lonely experience. It's as though I stand atop a mountain peak, exposed to harsh winds and temperatures. Many of the decisions and responsibilities I bear must be handled on my own. Much of the time, You are the only confidante I can turn to.

I take comfort as I look through the Scriptures and see the examples of great leaders like Moses and Daniel and Jesus. They knew what it was like to stand alone, be misunderstood, and criticized. Your prophets knew loneliness as well; their listeners mocked and rejected Your messages of warning. Yet You sustained all Your spokespeople as they kept their eyes fixed on You and their eternal reward.

May I keep my eyes fixed on You as well. Remind me that when I feel lonely, I'm not alone at all—You are my constant companion. I praise You for Your faithfulness.

The LORD your God, He is the One who goes with you.
He will not leave you nor forsake you.

DEUTERONOMY 31:6

WHEN REBUKE IS NECESSARY

Lord, when it comes to the need to discipline or rebuke someone, help me to move forward in a way that will bring about the best possible results. Even though a person is likely to be resistant or I'll become vulnerable to criticism, enable me with a loving boldness that is not afraid to speak and act.

For the sake of fairness, gift me with a wisdom that is impartial and examines all the facts. For the sake of making growth possible, enable me to be honest and ready with constructive suggestions. For the sake of interpersonal relations, may I be loving and thoughtful. And for the sake of bringing honor to You, may I cover the matter in prayer and conduct myself with integrity.

As I enact discipline, may I do so with humility. Help me to intertwine firmness with compassion. Be my guide every step of the way.

No chastening seems to be joyful for the present,
but painful; nevertheless, afterward it yields the
peaceable fruit of righteousness
to those who have been trained by it.

HEBREWS 12:11

Growing from Failure

Lord, Your grace and wisdom as a leader was abundantly on display when, after Peter denied You three times, You welcomed him to serve You again.

From Your example, I learn that failure doesn't have to be final—even when it is tragic. In spite of what Peter had done, You still chose to work through him. As You told the apostle Paul, Your power "works best in weakness" (2 Corinthians 12:9 NLT). It is through a humble vessel that You can shine the most.

When I am at fault, remind me that You are the God of second chances. When a member of my team at work fails and acknowledges it, lead me to handle the situation with the same kind of restorative grace You showed Peter.

Yes, there is much I can learn from failure. I want to be teachable so that I can grow in wisdom and humility. May I never take Your grace for granted!

Being confident of this very thing,
that He who has begun a good work in you
will complete it until the day of Jesus Christ.

PHILIPPIANS 1:6

TIME IS PRECIOUS

Lord, help me to view time as a precious commodity. Because it's limited, I need to be a careful steward of it. In every way—even in my rest and leisure, which also have value—I want to allot my hours wisely so that I am a productive and effective leader.

If I fail in the area of time management, I'm likely to fail elsewhere. I'll risk missing commitments and deadlines. I'll communicate to my followers that because time isn't important for me, it doesn't need to be important for them. Delays and procrastination are more likely. These all come with a high price—time that is forever lost.

Rather than look back with regret, I want to look forward with anticipation. Help me to weigh my options carefully so I can discern the best use of my time at any point in the day. I am eager to invest my hours in ways that please You and gain good returns.

LORD, remind me how brief my time on earth will be.
Remind me that my days are numbered—
how fleeting my life is.

PSALM 39:4 NLT

WHEN CRITICISM OVERWHELMS ME

Father, sometimes I feel as though multiple waves of disagreement or criticism are coming my way all at once. Usually the catalyst is a misunderstanding or a decision that was tough to make. The intensity of it all can get discouraging!

I want to be teachable when this happens. Maybe there is good reason for me to reconsider the cause of all the commotion. Could I have made a better decision or handled the matter more wisely? If so, help me to overcome any fear of admitting I might have been wrong.

But if I've exhausted all the options and what I did still needs to stand, may I take comfort in knowing I acted in integrity, and that You are fully aware of that. Free me from any need to defend myself. Instead, may I rest in Your vindication alone. Thank You for being my shield and protector.

He who dwells in the secret place of the Most High
Shall abide under the shadow of the Almighty.
I will say of the LORD, "He is my refuge and my fortress;
My God, in Him I will trust."

PSALM 91:1-2

The Power of Delegation

Lord, why is it that I'm reluctant to delegate? Though I have more than I can handle, what makes me resist the idea of giving a responsibility to another?

If it's because I fear yielding my power or authority to a follower, I show that I am lacking confidence and trust. If it's because I find myself intimidated by someone's outstanding skills and giftedness, help me to see that healthy growth can only take place when people are trusted with more, not less. If it's because I'm afraid the job won't get done right, awaken me to the opportunity to provide training and allow a person to rise to the challenge.

Help me to see that when I don't delegate, my own performance suffers. But when I gladly trust others and give the support they need, everyone benefits. You are the supreme example of delegation—You entrusted Your world-changing ministry to a ragtag group of disciples. And who can argue with the results made possible by Your empowerment?

He went up on the mountain and called to Him those He Himself wanted. And they came to Him. Then He appointed twelve, that they might be with Him and that He might send them out to preach.

MARK 3:13-14

Raising Up New Leaders

Lord, as I seek to raise up new leaders, help me to let go of expectations that might hinder people rather than help. Remind me that every person is gifted in unique ways, which means any attempt to clone myself or pursue a one-size-fits-all approach isn't going to work.

As I instruct and guide, help me to discern strengths I can nurture and weaknesses I can remedy. May I not be afraid to grant opportunities for new leaders to take on responsibilities that will stretch and demand more of them. May I just as freely entrust them to make their own decisions and take ownership of problems in need of solutions.

I realize this means careful planning and much patience on my part, for there's nothing accidental or automatic about training up good leaders. May I view this process not as a burden but a privilege! And fill me with a new gratefulness for the people who gladly poured themselves into me to make me the leader I am today.

Let us not grow weary while doing good,
for in due season we shall reap if we do not lose heart.

GALATIANS 6:9

PRAYER WISDOM

Prayer tells the truth about your faith in the power of God. It tells the truth about your relationship with God. Prayer tells the truth about our own sense of inadequacy or our feeling sense of competence before God. Prayer tells the truth about your love, your compassion, your fruitfulness, and your fight. We cannot rise much higher than our prayers.[20]

KEVIN DEYOUNG

MEASURING MY LEADERSHIP

Father, it is said a leader should take time every now and then to do a careful self-evaluation and ask, "How am I doing?" I see the wisdom of doing this—especially when I ask myself, "How do I measure up to the leadership of Jesus?"

Am I humble to the point of self-sacrifice, the kind that was willing to endure death on a cross? Do I yield to Your will and set aside my own? Do I pray before I make decisions, as Jesus did before choosing the Twelve? Am I patient in the same way Jesus was with those who were of little faith? Am I servant-hearted like the heavenly King who was willing to wash dirty feet? Do I give freely of wisdom and instruction, teaching and preparing people for bigger jobs ahead?

Thank You that as I look to Jesus, I can continue to grow and excel as a leader. Guide me as I seek to walk in His footsteps!

Be imitators of God, as beloved children. And walk in love,
as Christ loved us and gave himself up for us,
a fragrant offering and sacrifice to God.

EPHESIANS 5:1-2 ESV

My Challenges as a Leader

NOTES

1. J. Oswald Sanders, *Spiritual Leadership* (Chicago: Moody, 2007), 84-85.

2. Martyn Lloyd-Jones, *Studies in the Sermon on the Mount* (Grand Rapids, MI: Eerdmans, 1979), 2:45.

3. Elizabeth George, *A Woman After God's Own Heart* (Eugene, OR: Harvest House, 1997), 37.

4. Jeremiah Burroughs, *Gospel-Worship* (London: Printed for Peter Cole, 1648), 288. Minor edits were made to this text for clarity.

5. John Piper, "Ask Whatever You Wish," *Desiring God* (January 10, 1993), https://www.desiringgod.org/messages/ask-whatever-you-wish.

6. John MacArthur, *Lord, Teach Me to Pray* (Nashville: J. Countryman Books, 2003), 14-15 (emphasis added).

7. C.H. Spurgeon, *The Metropolitan Tabernacle Pulpit*, vol. 17 (London: Passmore & Alabaster, 1871), 689.

8. Octavius Winslow, *Personal Declension and Revival of Religion in the Soul* (New York: Robert Carter, 1848), 112-113.

9. D.L. Moody, *Prevailing Prayer: What Hinders It?* (Chicago: Fleming H. Revell, 1884), 102.

10. Stormie Omartian, *The Power of a Praying Life* (Eugene, OR: Harvest House, 2010), 15.

11. Timothy Keller, *Prayer* (New York: Viking, 2014), 18.

12. A.W. Tozer, *God Tells the Man Who Cares* (Chicago: Wingspread, 1993), 115-116. While these words were stated in the context of pastoral ministry, the principle can apply to all believers in their interactions with others.

13. Hannah More, *The Complete Works of Hannah More*, vol. II (New York: J.C. Derby, 1854), 515.

14. Thomas Watson, *The Godly Man's Picture* (Zeeland, MI: Reformed Church Publications, 2015), 70. Originally published in 1666.

15. H.B. Charles Jr., *It Happens After Prayer* (Chicago: Moody Publishers, 2013), 18-19.

16. Joni Eareckson Tada, *A Place of Healing* (Colorado Springs: David C. Cook, 2015), 40.

17. Jim George, *The Remarkable Prayers of the Bible* (Eugene, OR: Harvest House, 2006), 14.

18. J.I. Packer, *Knowing Christianity* (Downers Grove, IL: InterVarsity, 1999), 104.

19. C.H. Spurgeon, *Flashes of Thought* (London: Passmore & Alabaster, 1874), 319-320.

20. Kevin DeYoung, "Wrestling in Prayer," sermon at Christ Covenant Church, January 13, 2019, https://christcovenant.org/sermons/wrestling-in-prayer/.

ABOUT THE AUTHOR

Steve Miller is the author of *One-Minute Promises*, *One-Minute Praises*, *One-Minute Promises of Comfort*, *C.H. Spurgeon on Spiritual Leadership*, and *D.L. Moody on Spiritual Leadership*. With his wife, Becky, he is also the coauthor of the popular illustrated books *A Child's Garden of Prayer* and *101 Awesome Bible Puzzles for Kids*. Steve and Becky reside in Oregon's Willamette Valley and have three sons, two daughters-in-law, and grandchildren.